WHAT OTHERS ARE SAYING ABOUT ACKNOWLEDGMENT:

"ACKNOWLEDGMENT presents a practical methodology for recogni~~~~ ~~~ ~~~~~~~~~~~~~ ~~~~~~~~ ~~~ int~nse emo-tions of m

Herbe   ia

"ACKI   g grief
and loss.   nts especially h   grief."

Jan S   rnia

"I just   ing the
ocean th   ost my
son five y   loss—
not only i   warm.
I feel it c

Wive

"It alv   n word
has. I n   f time
is her   nakes
(the as
I fin   s: You
outline   nually
stress t   but essential.   ace to
start ar   want,
put (th   ey are
ready.
Tha   treme-
ly valu

Jar   Oregon

Acknow-ledgment

OPENING TO THE GRIEF OF UNACCEPTABLE LOSS

PETER LEECH, MSW, LCSW & ZEVA SINGER, MA, MFCC

ACKNOWLEDGMENT: *Opening to The Grief of Unacceptable Loss* is an original publication. Copyright ©1988 by Peter Leech & Zeva Singer, P.O. Box 1166, Laytonville, CA 95454.

ISBN 0-9620876-0-2

Library of Congress Catalog Card Number 88-51596

First Printing 1988
Second Printing 1989

Cover Design by Bruce McCloskey

Typeset by Barlow Typesetting, Inc.

Printed by Barlow Printing, Inc.

In Memory Of

Jacob Rueben Bloom

Dustin Steven Comer

David Henry Crews

James Alexander Farrell

Solomon Milton Bloom Garrido

Joshua Blue Maguire

Sarah Poxson Sparks

UNACCEPTABLE LOSS IS:

That loss that still brings you a lot of feeling,

after all these years;

That loss you still haven't been able to accept,

after all these tears;

That loss that still brings additional losses,

no matter how long it's been;

Any loss that continues to cause you to grieve,

if only once in a while.

    This book is for the survivors: we whose challenge it is to go on living in spite of catastrophic losses such as: the death of a loved one, life-threatening injury or illness, becoming physically disabled, being witness to catastrophic loss. It is not a book for everyone, however. If you have a way to manage your feelings about loss, and your life is going well with that approach, then you may not want this book, but you may want to pass it on to someone you know who can use it.
    If, however, you have sustained significant losses in your life and are wondering what to do with all the feelings, read on.

Acknowledgments

More people than I can count have helped me to find my path or made it easier to follow. I am especialy indebted to the following: Marcia Karp, M.A., Alex Quenk, Ph.D., and John Enright, Ph.D., who helped me rediscover myself through their patient—though relentless—therapeutic processes and personal kindnesses. Thanks to Sondra Reid for editing the early writings that became the framework of this book; our daughter, Jennifer, from whom I've learned the most about early childhood development; all those who allowed me to enter their lives during a time of catastrophic loss, and from whom I learned the basic principles of this approach; students and trainees whose feedback was invaluable in the development of exercises for the workbook; Joseph Knight for his tireless editing; and Zeva, without whose deep caring and energy this work would still be resting in a filing cabinet. *Peter Leech*

I would like to thank my students and clients who have been my best teachers; my children for being open and willing to talk to me about our past; Karen Loyster, who helped me confront the pain of receiving unconditional love; Herbert Lustig, M.D., who broke through my resistance to knowing my true history; Jan Smyth-Zeek for the encouragement to get this book ready for her fall classes on "Death and Dying"; and to Peter, for this amazingly simple way to work with the losses I have encountered in my life. He has lived the Acknowledgment Approach on a daily basis for longer than I have known him. It has been a privilege to work on this book with him. *Zeva Singer*

Photograph by Amy Frenzell

About The Authors

Peter Leech, M.S.W., is a Licensed Clinical Social Worker with twenty-five years of experience with individuals, families, and children, including extensive work with people who have sustained catastrophic loss. His personal experience with becoming disabled at age twenty-three has shaped his life personally and professionally, opening the way to the theory and practice of the Acknowledgment Approach. His professional experience includes teaching "The Psychology of Disability" at both the university and community college levels; he has been a group leader and has offered trainings and workshops on many subjects throughout his career, and he has been a consultant and trainer for numerous agencies.

Zeva Singer, M.A., is a Licensed Marriage and Family Therapist with fourteen years of experience. She has worked extensively with women who have experienced major relationship and/or career changes where depression and fear have markedly limited individual potential. Her specialities in private practice include "Inner Child" work designed to facilitate the working through of the grief of childhood losses so that a person can experience a return of the spontaneity, creativity, and spirituality of earlier years.

Both Peter and Zeva use hypnotherapy and psychotherapy in their practices. Over the years, they have offered numerous workshops and trainings on subjects related to the Acknowledgment Approach.

Table Of Contents

Introduction

Peter: This is a book that has been waiting to be written since 1976 when I presented a paper entitled "Emotional Responses in the Newly Disabled Adult" (The Psychiatric and Psychological Aspect of Disability Symposium; The Wright Institute; Berkeley, California).[1] In the years that followed, I received numerous requests for copies of my paper and was asked to provide a more comprehensive application of the principles to other forms of loss. More than once, I considered writing a book. However, it wasn't until Zeva and I joined our personal and professional lives in 1978 that I had the encouragement, cooperation, and the extra energy available to begin the actual writing.

In our professional lives, we have a joint private practice, working as a team when appropriate but continuing our independent work as well. For nearly fifteen years, we (individually and together) have been writing about loss. We've given pieces of our writing to our clients to use as information about loss and as worksheets to help them get a grasp on what is happening as they experience the intense emotions following what we refer to as an unacceptable loss. Our personal involvement has afforded us unlimited opportunity to use each other as consultants. Countless dinner hours, often extending into the night, have served as opportunities to discuss and evaluate our work with clients.

Although our conversations yielded more ways to explore each situation's uniqueness, we always concluded that the approach most basic to our work, and helpful to our clients, was that of working through the loss with a step-by-step, moment-to-moment acknowledgment of all the pieces. For this book, we have illustrated this approach by using material from our (combined) forty years of professional practice as well as events and experiences from our personal lives.

Zeva: My entrance into the professional field of counseling and psychotherapy was accomplished in the 1970s. I was divorced after a 24-year relationship; my children were teenagers, and I was finished with eight years of undergraduate and graduate schooling. I had relied heavily on therapy to help me get through the transitions, and I began to assess my need to contribute to a field from which I gained so much support.

My professional experience has included working with women going through major changes in their lives. From August, 1974, to February, 1980, I directed a counseling program that assisted literally thousands of "re-entry" women in their attempts to return to school. What I found was that most of these women were going through profound changes (rehabilitation after illness, injury, drug/alcohol abuse, divorce, death of a close friend, spouse, or family member), and the losses involved in the changes were life challenging. I felt unprepared to train the Women's Center staff to assist these students, and when I looked for further training, Peter's name was given to me as a potential consultant to the program. Finding that Peter's counseling approach worked well with women going through major changes in their lives, my staff and I began to employ his approach more and more, broadening our perspective on loss to include any significant change.

During the last four years, I've concentrated on the factors involving co-dependency. (In my opinion, co-dependency is living in a way that has you constantly re-adjusting your behavior—sometimes to extremes—to meet what you think are another person's needs. One's true self is abandoned in the process.) My personal work around the theme of shame in co-dependency is contained in Chapter Six.

The Lifeline in Chapter 8 has been used in my teaching over the past 14 years, and it is specific to my interest in "getting personal history straight" as a prerequisite to working through childhood/young adult/adult losses. The process for my own recovery has relied heavily on the Acknowledgment Approach.

Peter: My personal experience includes becoming physically disabled by polio in 1956 when I was 23 years old. My professional experience, beginning in graduate school in the early 1960's, has been focused, shaped, and examined in the light of my personal experience, and vice versa. I know I brought good training and intuition into my first hospital/physical rehab center job, but I was concerned that some patients gradually deteriorated and often died, and my hunch was that their deterioration had nothing to do with their original injury or illness. I could see that they were depressed, and I believed that their deterioration had to do with their depression, but I did not trust that I had anything to offer them. I searched for approaches different from those offered in graduate training—ostensibly so I could become more effective in my work.

In psychodramatic training, I found my anger, and with its release, an incredible energy filled my body—such contrast to the low energy level to which I had become accustomed. I was startled to find I had been depressed; the energy return was available only because I connected with my feelings. My search had led me to grow, and my work grew accordingly. I realized that, contrary to the textbooks and my previous experience with psychotherapy, I did not have to be depressed in order to continue to live with a disability.

In later Gestalt work, I focused my thinking about my life and my work in ways that helped make sense out of the things I had been doing. Since my own hospitalization, I'd been puzzled and troubled by the fact that I didn't (and still don't) accept being physically limited. The "awareness" approach prompted me to question what I had been doing if not accepting. My answer was that I, at least, was acknowledging that I had become physically limited: I started using a wheelchair for mobility; I had extensive physical therapy and hand reconstruction; I "let go" of being a photographer and went to college to begin a new career; I learned to drive with hand controls, built ramps to my house—all constructive responses to my limitations. All of this was possible only because I had carefully examined my losses, my needs, my strengths, and my feelings, and because I had acknowledged everything this meant to my life. I had reclaimed my power and put my energy into rebuilding my life.

I was encouraged by my own work to push for the feelings in those people I saw who were depressed. My way of talking and working with people about loss and grief included the Acknowledgment Approach more and more as I came to see that it was the most effective way to deal with depression. I believe even more strongly now, after many thousands of hours of successful work with people who have sustained catastrophic loss, that the approach that acknowledges the loss in detail and all the feelings stimulated by that loss is the least oppressive and most constructive.

CHAPTER ONE

Opening to the Grief

Waves of grief
Dwarfing the tides
Giant waves along the Mendocino Coast

No way to know when they're coming
Nor what calls them

The physical pain of holding back the waves
The wrenching release as they wash over you
Quiet exhaustion
As they gather their energy

There can be no plan for this
There can be only readiness . . .

Feelings surface
Feelings flow
Releasing pain
Releasing you from the undertow of your grief

The loss of life as you have known it can take many forms. It may occur in the form of the death of a loved one: a parent, a partner, a child—even a pet that has become a part of your life.

It may take the form of the anticipated death, (due to a serious illness) of yourself or someone you love.

It could present itself through your becoming physically disabled: the loss of your life as a physically unlimited person.

It may occur as the end of a relationship, which includes both the loss of a person and the loss of your dream of life as a person in a permanent relationship.

The examples are endless and unique to each person's experience. Loss, however, is the element common to all grief.

The emotions contained in your grief include deep sadness, intense anger, paralyzing fear, perhaps debilitating guilt or shame. They will not come to you neatly packaged in outline form; they will come all at once, like waves, with an intensity that cannot be anticipated. The magnitude of your response will be in direct proportion to the magnitude of your loss; that is, the more you care about some part of your life—the stronger your connection and involvement is—the more intense will be your response if you lose it. These are the waves of grief that take you by surprise.

Because loss is so personal, you are the only one who can define whether a loss is significant and to what degree. A significant loss is like a wound in your personal universe, creating a gap or hole in your daily life. A disorientation follows that changes your perspective on anything and everything you encounter. It's as if you've awakened in an alien land. You may feel similar to what is described in "The Whirlpool Experience:"[2]

> *Feeling you are falling apart*
> *Feeling you are going crazy*
> *Feeling you are disappearing*
> *Feeling you are in limbo*
> *Feeling you are out of control*
> *Feeling of disorientation*
> *Feeling of total confusion*
> *Your whole body shakes*
> *Feeling totally abandoned, all alone*
> *Feeling, thinking no one cares . . .*

Too often, people we trust—ministers, parents, teachers, respected friends—tell us that we are grieving too long, and that if we just "accept" the loss, we will "feel better." Perhaps that means we will somehow feel less sad, angry, or fearful of future losses. We do our best to follow the advice, but when the feelings re-surface, we may feel frightened or guilty because we haven't "accepted" what has happened, and we're back in the grieving process. For the most part, we feel confused or troubled about our inability to truly accept our loss. After a time, we feel burdened by the expectation and may even begin to ask, "Why can't I accept this?"

A better question to ask is, "What about this loss is acceptable to me?" The usual answer is "None of it!"

"If it's not acceptable, then why should you accept it?"

"You mean I have a choice?"

"Yes. You don't have to accept anything—especially something so tragic."

When we give our clients this permission, they nearly always are flooded with tears of relief: relief at not having to do the impossible. It is permission to feel, to open to all that is, but not to force acceptance when it isn't possible.

What does it mean to "accept" a loss? Does it mean to "pretend I never had what I've lost so I won't have any feelings about losing it?" Or does it mean that "I should start liking the fact that I've sustained this loss? Can I learn to like it that my friend or child has died? Or that I've lost my job or become physically damaged in some way?"

Acceptance is totally contradictory to the usual expectation that we care about ourselves and other people; it expects us to stop caring and, therefore, it's confusing. That's why there is often great relief in coming to realize that many losses are unacceptable.

How long does it take to "get over a loss?" That depends upon the nature of the loss and what all of the related losses might be. In actuality, you won't "get over" a significant loss. Your relationship to it will change after working through the feelings, and you will become aware that the loss has ceased to be the primary preoccupation in your life.

The authors believe that the only way to work through the most extreme part of the grief is to explore the wound that loss prompts in the same way that you would explore a wound of the flesh.

How long is it? How wide? How deep?
What vital parts does it touch?
Is it a clean cut? Or a jagged tear? A puncture?
Is there anything in it? Is it bleeding?
Where does it hurt? How does it hurt?
How long ago did this happen? What did you do?
Will it affect your function? Will it heal?
What scars will you have? How will they look?
What are you feeling? Are you afraid? Of what?

Time does not heal wounds without acknowledgment of what has happened. You need to clarify your feelings and express them in a way that defines in detail what you have lost, how much you care about what you have lost, and the value of what you have left. Knowing what you miss about a person who has died will help honor the person and the place s/he had in your life. Acknowledgment is the process of coming to that knowing. Acknowledgment is the process of seeing things as they are, not as they "should" or "shouldn't" be. It is recognizing "what is" for you at any moment in time. It includes a recognition of the external reality factors affecting your life, your beliefs, your bodily sensations, your thoughts, and your emotions (feelings). It also includes the recognition of the possibility of change: that is, any of the above may change from moment to moment, day to day, week to week, year to year, and so on.

The goal of the acknowledgment process is to become completely re-acquainted and re-connected with yourself and your universe in a way that allows the loss to assume whatever proportions are appropriate when considered in relation to all other facets of your life. There can be no comparing of your experience with any one else's. It's your personal response to any event that is unique because only you know what you are experiencing, and you are the only person who can come to this knowing of yourself. No one else can tell you what you should or shouldn't feel.

There is more to "The Whirlpool Experience":

"The Whirlpool Experience" is not tragedy.
The events of life are neutral,

And tragedy is when you allow the events of life
To stop you from continuing to fulfill
The person you were created to be
And you start dying
And that's tragedy.

No matter what the nature of the event, it is our response to it that can shape our lives. For one person, the death of a son might mean life is over. For another, it might mean a more spiritual or religious conviction; for a third, a dedication to helping other parents. While we think it is useful to describe the event as specifically as possible, we suggest your attention go to focusing on your emotional response, concentrating on the process of acknowledgment.

There is no test more rigorous of whether or not our early learning has prepared us to respond constructively to the challenges of adult life than the experience of catastrophic loss. It is in this arena that we offer this book and the process of acknowledgment as a tool useful in responding to the most profound of life's challenges.

THE WORKBOOK:
GENERAL INSTRUCTIONS

At the end of each chapter, we have included a "workbook" section that will guide you in your work on the feelings described in that chapter. You will see that as you work from chapter to chapter there is some repetition. This is due to the fact that in one moment one feeling will arise, and the next moment another feeling will arise, and so on. The purpose of the workbook is to elicit all the details and feelings about the loss, specifying even the minute, often forgotten or embarrassing thoughts. We believe that all the things that a person feels or thinks about a loss are important. We have learned that writing down the details gets them out of your head and makes them much more tangible, aiding in their acknowledgment.

THE USE OF A JOURNAL

We suggest that you keep your work in a personal journal so that you will have all your notes, lists, and comments in one place to refer back to as you work along. If you don't have a notebook to start with right now, just begin on some blank pieces of paper. You can paste them into your journal later on.

TIME FOR YOURSELF

Let the people you live with know that you are doing some important work for yourself and request uninterrupted time. If you have a supportive friend or family member, ask that person just to be there. S/he doesn't have to do anything—including "making you feel better"—when your work brings your feelings to the surface.

Note what happens after you express all your feelings: the energy that has been holding down the feelings will release. If you continue with this expression, you will begin to feel lighter and more energized. You will experience a period of relief and, while nothing is changed—what you lost still is lost to you—you will have a perspective on your feelings and energy to put into some other part of your life.

PERSONALIZING

The idea behind personalizing is to make the experience *yours* by focusing your attention on *your* feelings. At some later date, it may be useful for you to generalize, but for now, use "I" statements such as "I lost. . .," "I lose. . .," "I feel sad because. . .," "I am angry about. . .," "I am afraid of. . . ." If you have no name for a particular feeling, you can say, "I feel knots in my stomach," "I feel a tightness in my throat," etc.

BEING SPECIFIC

The idea behind being specific is, again, to focus your attention on *your* experience, only this time, the focus is on each small component of that experience. You may indeed have "lost everything," but that "everything" is made up of many components. In like manner, you may be angry about or afraid of "everything," and you can slice "everything" so thinly that you specify each detail. *Every piece of the experience is important and must be acknowledged.* When you have done that, you will know exactly what it is that you have to deal with.

RELAXED BREATHING

Before and after each period of work with the workbook, take a few minutes to do some relaxed breathing. Sit in a relaxed breathing position that is comfortable for you. Take a deep breath and let it flow completely out. Repeat twice. It's OK to make a noise as you let your breath out. This will serve to relax you more. You can imagine that you are using your breath as a grounding force, thinking of your exhale as a silver cord that begins up above your head and follows your spinal column, splitting to go down your legs and into your feet. Imagine that cord, through the exhale, extending out of your body, through the soles of your feet and the base of your spine, and going down into the earth below. Each exhale can take it deeper until you can imagine it embedding in the deepest part of the earth. Then you can allow your inhales to bring energy up from the earth into your body. Let the energy be like fluid, filling your body with its grounding, calming effect. This will help get you focused, preparing you for the next step.

FOCUSING ON YOUR LOSS

On the first fresh page of your journal, write a simple word or phrase that represents the primary loss you are working on now. This may be a recent loss, or it may not be. If you are not currently feeling any grief and want to understand this process better, choose any loss out of your past to use as your example.

NOTES

CHAPTER TWO

Grief

"Grief" and "mourning" are words that are commonly used to describe our emotional state following a loss. As concepts, both words seem to summarize all that we experience. Too often, however, these words are used to "explain" some of our responses without an attempt to understand more precisely what is going on. Perhaps you've heard, "Oh, she's just grieving," or "He's still in his mourning period."

These phrases have an element of truth to them, but tend to diminish the importance of grief, or dismiss it as something that needs little attention.

"Grief" is the collection of emotional responses, or feelings, that follow a significant loss. It is possible to break down the experience of grief into its component parts so that you can understand more clearly what is happening when you are immersed in grief. It is necessary to do this so that you can encourage the passage through grief. To do anything less is interruptive of grief and contributes to your becoming depressed.

MORE THAN SADNESS

Contrary to popular usage, grief is something more than just sadness. It actually consists of a variety of emotions, many of which are unique to the individual and the nature of the loss. There are, however, a few that occur consistently, are poorly understood and, therefore, might be troublesome:

shock,
   sadness,
      anger,
         guilt,
            shame,
               fear.

These emotions or feelings can arise with such force that you may become frightened by their energy and, having little if any experience in dealing with such feelings, you may do your best to suppress them. You may think the feelings are negative and likely to be unacceptable. You may also get a lot of encouragement to continue to suppress your feelings from people around you who also have limited experience and are uncomfortable with these particular feelings or their intensity.

In the following pages, we will take each of these feelings in turn, describe their nature and function in detail, outline some of the pitfalls associated with each, and provide some direct guidance for you to work your way through them. In so doing, we'll also provide some basic groundwork for you to use to sort out any other feelings about your loss that may be unique to you as an individual or to your situation of loss.

FEELINGS BEGIN IN YOUR BODY

Emotions (or feelings) begin with a body sensation: a fullness in your heart, throat, or face; build-up of tears in your eyes; tightness in your throat, solar plexus, or back; nausea, cramping; a "sinking" sensation; breathlessness, dizziness, etc. First descriptions of feelings often use the bodily sensation as a focus:

"I am numb, heavy." "There's a lump in my throat." "I can hardly breathe." "I have butterflies in my stomach." "There's a pain in my chest." You may be able to come up with a "label" for a certain grouping of these bodily sensations, such as anger, sadness, fear, guilt, shame, etc. On the other hand, you may not be able to label the feelings that come up around a profound loss. Many of us come from families where the modeling of our parents did not reflect adequate or appropriate responses to loss. Grieving was hidden, or the feelings that would arise around losses were discouraged or invalidated, so that we learned early in life to suppress certain feelings. While bodily sensations move with the speed of light, your intellect is quick, too, and you may have learned to immediately block what you were experiencing.

IF I DIDN'T CARE. . .

In addition, the intensity of the emotion that arises in response to a profound loss may surprise or even frighten you. You may begin to think you're "falling apart," "going to pieces," or "going crazy" because you can't manage these feelings in the same way you have managed the feelings associated with minor losses. The intensity of your emotions will be directly related to the degree you care about whatever you've lost. The more you care, the more feeling you will have.

For example, for you as an adult to lose a penny or two is hardly worth more than a shrug. If your child loses cherished pennies it can be a big loss. For you to lose a quarter may not matter much, depending on the circumstances. If it is your only quarter, and you were about to put it into the pay phone to call a tow truck because your car is broken down on a dark and stormy night, it will have great significance for you. The loss of your car keys or your wallet may bring a burst of feelings—worry, annoyance, frustration—that dissipates as soon as you find or replace these things.

The loss of someone you love is of a totally different magnitude; your feelings about this loss will reach an intensity that will astound you until you begin to understand clearly what is happening and what the basis for the intensity is. Another factor that will contribute to the intensity of the feelings is that a current situation will bring up the feelings about previous losses. You may not recognize that this is happening early on as you are preoccupied with the recent loss. As you continue to sort out your feelings, you will begin to clarify whether the current loss or a past loss is the source.

WHAT IS LOSS?

Here are some losses that we begin to encounter as children that have a counterpart in adult life:

Loss of a favorite toy
Dropping an ice cream cone in the dirt
Not receiving an anticipated gift
A friend starts playing with someone else
Parents decide to move away from
the familiar neighborhood
A pet gets lost or dies.

Some adult counterparts:

Loss of a job/retirement/aging
Job change that is not anticipated
Abortion/miscarriage/stillbirth
Giving a child up for adoption
Separation/divorce
Children leaving home
Move to another city
Physical illness/injury/disability
Terminal illness of a child, friend, parent, lover
Death of a child, friend, parent, partner, pet.

We all have had the experience of being told by someone else that our loss is not important enough to make "such a fuss about." This is often a part of our early learning about loss: that our loss is not as important as someone else's. It is very important that children be encouraged to attend to the losses they experience as significant events in their lives. Then they can be prepared to respond constructively to the losses they will inevitably encounter as they grow up. In question/answer sessions after a presentation about loss, we've often heard someone ask, "How can I understand what that person is feeling regarding his/her loss when I have never experienced anything like that?"

We suggest that you have experienced something similar, but that you very likely learned to diminish its importance and now believe that you haven't experienced loss at all. A quick glance over the preceeding list may give you a clue about some loss you have experienced. The magnitude of the loss may be different, but the feelings are very likely similar.

PRIMARY AND SECONDARY LOSSES

Primary loss is the most obvious, and the one that draws the focus; secondary losses are those that occur as a direct result of the primary loss, although they may not even be apparent or seem important at the outset. Indeed, one characteristic of secondary losses is that they make their appearance over a period of time. Just when everyone else is thinking that a person's mourning period is past, a new, secondary loss becomes apparent, and the grieving person is plunged back into grief. Another characteristic of secondary losses is that there is no way for anyone to anticipate what all of the secondary losses will be.

There is one secondary loss, however, that occurs consistently. This is the loss of the sense of support and closeness if family members and friends do not acknowledge and validate intense feelings. Take, for example, parents who have lost a child: too often they tend to hide their grief from one another, believing that "If I cry, it will make my partner cry, so I'll only cry when I'm alone." Since both are grieving, then both must physically hide from the other in order to express their feeling, and the result is that they become distant from one another. Each begins to feel estranged—a secondary loss—at a time when they need each other the most.

For the most part, secondary loss is a very individualized experience. Peter lists some of the secondary losses related to his becoming physically disabled.

In the first years after becoming disabled, they were:

Loss of my ability to work as a photographer
Loss of my ability to earn an income
Loss of my ability to provide for my family
Loss of my sense of myself as a man who provides
Loss of my sense of being an independent person.

In later years they became:

> Loss of being able to travel freely
> Loss of the time it takes me to get ready
> to go in the morning
> Continual struggle with architectural barriers.

For some, secondary loss may very closely parallel the primary loss. For others, it may be more far-reaching than anyone could ever imagine. This is not to say that it is necessary to go searching for secondary losses if they are not apparent. They must, however, be recognized as they appear and be considered as an integral part of an individual's grieving process.

HOW CAN I EVER DEAL WITH ALL OF THIS?

There are a number of different approaches to dealing with grief in this society that are quite common. They seem to support the prevalent myth that intense emotion of the "negative" variety is unacceptable, especially in public—that is, within view of any other human being. It is all right to express "positive" emotions such as joy, happiness, elation at winning at a game or being a supporter of a winning team, getting married, having a (healthy) baby. Death and other significant losses are, for the most part, dealt with in silence or embarrassment if some extreme sign of grief (such as an over-abundance of tears or intense anger) slips out.

When you were a child, your entire universe was represented by the small sub-culture in which you grew up. The approaches you learned from that culture for managing grief can keep you out of trouble most of the time—as long as your losses are simple and few. As your losses become more significant, you may feel confused as you reach for the old approach and find it doesn't work. Most people just double their efforts when something doesn't work, but if you double your efforts with an approach that is already inadequate and insufficient to deal with the overwhelming challenge facing you, your confusion and pain will increase, and you may not be able to avoid depression.

Here are three commonly used approaches for managing

grief that are ineffective when you are attempting to deal with a major loss:

Avoidance (of the feelings surrounding loss): The basic strategy in the "Avoidance Approach" is to stay away from people, places, events, or anything that will serve as a reminder of the loss. Being reminded of the loss will, of course, cause some feelings to arise about it. Avoidance is the remedy that keeps feelings away. One drawback, though, is that when you avoid the people, places, and events that were a part of the life that was related to the loss, it means you are avoiding your family, friends, places you go, things you do, music you hear, etc., and this results in significant secondary losses for you. You might want to try the second approach.

Pretend-you-never-had-anything is an approach that employs a slightly different strategy. If you didn't have something, you can't experience any loss of it. So if you pretend that you didn't have the person that you lost, you can avoid any expression of grief for that person. This allows you to associate with family and friends, go and do your usual things as long as no one mentions the name of the deceased or slips and makes some reference that will call attention to the absence. This slows down the conversation a bit, but, since almost everyone is practiced at this approach, no one minds very much. If someone does slip up or otherwise contributes to feelings beginning to arise, a third approach can be tried.

The Platitudinous Approach is one that allows us to talk about the loss without revealing any feeling. You're probably familiar with at least a few of these sayings:

"Oh, everyone has to go sometime."
"Boy, that's the way to go, isn't it? Bang; like that!"
"No use crying over spilt milk."
"Well, she's much happier now."
"Every cloud has a silver lining."
"Just have to keep a stiff upper lip."
"You just have to accept these things and everything will be all right."

ACKNOWLEDGMENT: OPENING TO THE GRIEF

It is easy to find an alternative to the above three approaches; just watch young children respond to their world. The act of acknowledgment is not new; small children do it all the time. There is a period of time in early childhood when we are willing to acknowledge what we are feeling, thinking, and wanting on a moment-to-moment basis, and we aren't afraid to tell the people around us about it one way or another.

Children will react spontaneously to being hurt unless or until a parent or other model tries to shape their behavior for societal, cultural, or personal reasons.

Inherent in your genes was a driving force to find a model that would appropriately show you how to relate to the world at your different stages of development.[3] Of course, loss is a part of the world, and your model showed you his/her ways to respond to loss. If you lacked the kind of model that acknowledged loss and all the accompanying feelings, you were caught between naturally reacting with emotional response and being punished for doing so. Most of us were rewarded and punished by the same people; we wanted to please, and we became hypersensitive to responses that either supported us ("You make me so happy when you do those things.") or negated us ("You cause me embarrassment by the way you act").

If we made a statement about our feelings to someone who was uncomfortable about intense feelings, we may have been told:

"That's silly."
"You're making that up."
"You shouldn't feel that way."
"You're selfish."
"Don't cry over spilt milk."
"We'll get you another one; just stop crying."
"Forget all about that; come and have a cookie."

And we learned our lessons well. So well, in fact, that we just took for granted that the only way to be in the world was to suppress our intense feelings. As we grew older, we learned to be cautious about acknowledgments. We realized that we were dependent upon the people around us for just about everything, and we decided we had better "comply" with what they said we should or shouldn't do. Some of us even ceased to be aware that we felt, thought, or wanted certain things if the pressure was strong enough.

Remember that we, as children, are genetically coded to find and follow our models.[3] You can see that if our models cover up their feelings and disregard ours, we will be compelled to do the same until we decide to break the cycle. We can come to a new understanding and a new behavior even if our previous models were not able to show us healthy methods to deal with catastrophic loss.

The idea, then, is to:

Open ourselves to the wisdom of small children;
Open ourselves to the feelings;
Open ourselves to expression of them;
Open to the grief;
Open to an acknowledgment of the loss;
Open to all of the feelings we have about it;
Open to everything it implies about our present and future life.

As we continue over time to acknowledge everything we've lost and everything we have left, we can begin to make specific plans about how to proceed with our lives. Through this process of acknowledgment, we gradually grow to a new acceptance of ourselves as survivors of catastrophic loss.

There are some characteristics of the Acknowledgment Approach that are essential to its effective use. One of these has to do with personalizing your thinking about your experience. Because your loss is very personal, your grief is also very personal. It is essential that you use "I" statements. "I feel...," "I think...," "I want...," will be much more useful to you than, "people feel...," "people think...," "people want...," or the collectives "you" or "they" in reference to your experience.

Another essential characteristic of the acknowledgment process is that of being specific about your experience.

Again, the experience of loss is very personal and specifically yours. You will become much more meaningfully related to exactly what you have lost—and ultimately what you have left—if your references are to the specifics of your loss. If I say to you, 'I have lost everything,' it will have meaning for you only in terms of what it might mean to you to "lose everything." It will convey nothing of my loss. Even if there may be times when you will choose to be non-specific with another person for your own reasons, it will be much more useful in your personal work if you allow yourself to become aware of the specific nature of your primary and secondary losses.

A third essential feature of this approach involves your careful distinction between your thoughts (beliefs) and your feelings (emotions). Both are valuable and deserve equal time; however, if they are not distinguished one from the other, the results are often confusing. You may think that you are dealing with the feelings when you include the word "feel" in a statement. For example, someone may say, "I feel that a mature person shouldn't cry."

This is a statement of belief or thought, not a statement of feeling. A more accurate statement of the belief might be, "I believe that a mature person shouldn't cry."

If, in fact, the person wishes to state a feeling, s/he could say, "I feel uncomfortable when I see a mature person cry."

This, now, uses the idea that feelings/emotions begin as body sensations and clearly represents what the speaker is feeling. Likewise, "I feel sad," is much clearer than, "I feel that a person should be sad about this."

The distinction is important in that if you're only talking about your beliefs or thoughts, you're not getting down to the grief. Just using the word "feel" is not enough; you must get to the feelings.

THE WORKBOOK:
IDENTIFYING FEELINGS

Remember to have your writing materials handy as you take some time for yourself to work in the workbook. Sit comfortably and get relaxed as you do some deep breathing before beginning the exercise.

Now, let your mind focus on the primary loss you are currently working on or one that you wish to select from previous losses. Let an image of that which is lost to you arise; it may be an image of a person, of doing something with that person, of doing something that you can no longer do, etc. As the image arises, pay attention to any of the feelings that begin to stir anywhere in your body: any change in your muscles, tightening or loosening, any change in your breathing, constrictions in your gut, throat or face. Take a few minutes to explore these, to get acquainted with whatever they are, and then take all the time you need to write down whatever collection of feeling seems to fit.

Use the following headings:

stressfulness

loss/sadness

hurt/anger

guilt/shame

vulnerability/fear

As you continue through the workbook, remember to add to the lists as you become acquainted with new feelings.

CHAPTER THREE

Interrupted Grief & Depression

The thing that is problematic for many people is not that they are grieving, but that they are not grieving. Often this is because someone has interrupted them. What does it mean to interrupt grief? It means to interfere with the process, to distract from feeling by changing the subject, taking your mind off a particular thought, or, perhaps, pretending as though nothing is happening. You may discount the intensity of loss or feeling or call such feelings "bad" feelings. Sometimes you may choose to defer your feelings (interrupting your grief) because you are facilitating someone else's process. Be aware that whenever you interrupt your grief, you court depression.

Grief is often interrupted under the guise of making you "feel better," that is, someone convinces you to stop crying or asks you not to reveal your feelings of sadness, anger, fear, or guilt. Sometimes people are encouraged to use drugs (prescribed or not) such as tranquilizers, mood-elevators, sleeping pills, alcohol, etc., and most drugs effectively interrupt grief. Family members or friends may suggest distractions such as: "Let's go to a movie," "Let's go out to dinner," "Why don't we go shopping?" "You'll feel better once you get cleaned up, shaved," "Why not get a permanent?"

There may be admonitions that you're not doing it right: "Why are you dwelling on this?" "That's just self-pity," "You're just wallowing in your pain," "You should be over this by now," "You shouldn't be thinking about that." When someone says you "should" be doing something, you know you aren't, and if they say you "shouldn't" be doing something, you know you are. If you aren't "getting over" this loss, you must be doing something else. So let's just look at "what is" and not complicate things.

People who want to interrupt your grief may be well intentioned, but they are wanting you to stop expressing your feelings so they will feel better. You see, it's so difficult for some people to feel their feelings that they will do anything to prevent you from feeling yours so that they won't feel theirs.

Any and all of these interruptions have the effect of invalidating you and your feelings, as if you are wrong or inappropriate. This, coming at a time when you already feel vulnerable to further loss, may cause you to suppress your feelings (interrupt your grief) in order not to risk losing the support of family, friends, and professionals whose help you are seeking.

One thing that is problematic about interrupting grief is that the interruption interferes with the awareness of loss necessary for you to maintain control over your own life. You must look at your wound in order to know what to do about it. But if, for example, you are interrupted every time you begin to explore and feel your loss, then you never will be able to consider your primary and secondary losses in detail. If you are prevented from knowing what you feel about your losses, you never will have the information you need to make the decisions and plans necessary to deal effectively with your life. This leaves you vulnerable to making decisions by default or to becoming dependent on others to make decisions for you; either one of these are additional secondary losses to add to your storehouse of grief.

DEPRESSION IS NOT A SEQUELA TO LOSS

Of even greater importance is the fact that interrupting grief will contribute to your becoming depressed. In all our experience, we've found that depression is not a natural sequela to loss. It is the result of the suppression of feelings such as anger, sadness, fear, guilt, shame, etc. We consciously suppress our feelings if we've learned that it's not acceptable to reveal them. This "holding down" of feelings requires an expenditure of energy: the more powerful the feelings, i.e., the more you care about the event, the greater will be the amount of energy required to suppress the feelings. Less energy is then available for usual activities, and the result is to feel "depressed." If you can imagine the energy associated with the full intensity of your sadness and your anger and your fears, and then imagine the amount of energy it would require to suppress all those feelings, you will have an idea of the amount of energy not available to expend on daily life.

Sometimes depression is hard to recognize because a person may be agitated, creating work in order to fill up time so there is little opportunity to experience feelings. This is most often characteristic of people who are caught up in the "post-traumatic stress cycle" (Chapter Four). In either case, there is no expression of true emotion.

DEPRESSION OR SADNESS?

The concept that depression need not occur after a loss may come as a surprise to you. This is not to say that depression does not occur. Of course it does. It is to say that depression need not occur when all the other components of grief—the sadness, anger, guilt, fear—are fully acknowledged and honored from the outset. There will be sadness, lots and lots of sadness, but not depression.

The distinction between "sadness" and "depression" is more than semantic. An expression of sadness, with accompanying tears, no matter how deep and/or profound, is relieving and cleansing when working through a loss: it is followed by a period in which people have said they feel "easier," "less physical pain," having "more clarity about what to do."

Depression, on the other hand, is a totally different experience characterized by an absence of feeling: "I'm just numb," "I don't feel anything." There is a profound loss of energy, disinterest in life, inability to function, and, what is most dangerous, an inability of one's body to resist illness or to heal itself.

It is this last part that originally caused Peter's concern about depression. In his early work in a physical rehabilitation center, he began to see that people who could not resolve their depression about their physical losses became more ill, acquired more secondary infections, and often died. An example of a situation in which interrupted grief resulted in depression may serve to illustrate this.

DEPRESSION COMPLICATES ILLNESS

Peter: I was asked to see a woman, whom I'll call "G", who was newly admitted to a physical rehab unit in a Bay Area hospital in serious condition because of pressure sores that had eroded much of her buttocks from one hip around to the other hip. She was being treated in isolation to avoid infection, was seen as depressed, and, because of the seriousness of her condition, the supervising nurse believed I should see her as soon as possible.

The brief history I got out of G's record before seeing her indicated that she had been functioning fairly well for some years with a diagnosis of multiple sclerosis. She was employed, and she was a single parent, caring adequately for two children aged seven and nine. About six months prior to my being called, G had had a sudden progression of her MS that had caused her to lose both motor and sensory function in her lower extremities. This primarily affected her ability to walk but also caused her to be unable to feel pressure.

In response to this crisis, G's friends acquired a wheelchair for her so that she could continue to work. They apparently did not understand, however, her need for a cushion, and because of her inability to feel pressure, she developed pressure sores on her buttocks in a very short while. She took some time off work to treat the sores. However, healing pressure sores is a very slow process and within a few weeks it was apparent she could not continue to work. She lost her job and her income. When it came time to pay her rent, she had no money and so agreed with the landlord that she would have to move. Friends and, I believe, a local church helped her to move into a smaller apartment that she could afford on the disability benefits that someone had helped her apply for, but the apartment could not be ramped for her to get in and out of, and she apparently could not get into the bathroom with her wheelchair.

At this time, a public health nurse began to visit G and tried to help with the pressure sores that, because of the difficulty with bathing and such, had become infected. The PHN also described G as being depressed. Shortly after this she became ill with the "flu" and spent two weeks or so in bed in a slow recovery, probably due to both her MS and her depression. As a result of the time in bed, she had developed pressure sores on both hips and, in spite of the PHN's frequent assistance, they too soon became infected. The PHN continued to describe her as very depressed.

At about this time a county social worker made a home visit in connection with the disability benefits and became concerned that G was unable to adequately care for her children; however, instead of investigating local or family placement possibilities, she quickly arranged for out-of-home placement in the county's facility for dependent children. The PHN continued to describe G as "very depressed," and treatment for her pressure sores had no healing effect. Over the next four to six weeks prior to admission, the sores gradually worsened and merged. They were the precipitating cause for her hospital admission. G was described after admission as being "depressed" and unwilling to respond to anyone in other than monosyllabic answers to questions.

Because G was being treated in an isolation room to guard against further infection, my wheelchair and I had to get scrubbed and gowned to enable me to go in to talk with her. After being introduced by the nurse, I feigned ignorance of the historical information I had so that I could ask G to tell me her story. "It looks to me as though you are in quite a mess," I acknowledged. "Can you tell me how this got started?"

G started slowly, but as I asked for more information, she complied and gradually filled in the details of the story outlined above. When she got to the part about her children being "taken away," I asked, "Doesn't any of this make you feel angry?"

With the first burst of energy I'd seen since we began to talk, she said, with her eyes snapping with fire, "Yes, I'm real angry about them taking my children away like that. They could at least have let them stay with their Auntie who lives nearby. I haven't even seen them in I-don't-know-how-long. I can't stand it that they're in that "jail-house"; they didn't do anything wrong. Why, they only tried to help me when I needed it!"

And with that, we began to discuss in considerable detail some of the other things G had felt angry about during this whole ordeal, some of the things she felt saddest about, and finally, what could be done to get her children into a placement with their aunt, G's sister, since this was the focus of highest energy for her. At one point a nurse came in to see what had happened to me and this woman who "wouldn't talk to anyone."

After an hour-and-a-half with her, I left G with the promise that I would make calls to the social worker and her sister and, if anything could be done to get her children out of the county facility, I would see to it that the process got started. G told me that she was glad to have a chance to talk to me and would look forward to seeing me again. She seemed in much higher spirits than at the beginning of our time together or in anything I had read about her.

It took the next two days with messages back and forth for me to complete the call to the social worker. G's sister was agreeable to having the children and glad to have someone help make it happen. The social worker, too, could find no reason other than red tape to detain the children and said she would move as quickly as possible to make the required home visit and get things started. I called back the third day to arrange to see G again and was appalled to hear that it was too late. G had died the day before due to the blood-poisoning from her massive wound infection.

MS, at the stage described in the above example, is not, in and of itself, a fatal illness. The depression, allowed to go on without intervention for so long, was the deciding factor in this woman's body reaching the point of no return. Depression, we repeat, is not a natural sequela to any loss. If depression is seen only as something to expect, to sympathize with, rather than being a potential danger to the person's survival, we may, by "being supportive" of a person's depressive process, inadvertently contribute to the development of secondary illness that could very well endanger their lives.

SUPPRESSED FEELING ABOUT IMMINENT DEATH

Here are two examples of interrupted grief in Zeva's personal history:

Zeva: In 1972 my family was insistent that my father not know he was dying. They believed it would be too painful for him to know, so we spent hours not talking about it. "Just be cheerful. Bring the children and some kind of a gift." "Maybe you shouldn't see him now; he looks very bad, and you cry so much that it makes it hard to be with you." And at home, my husband and friends insisted that I not call to talk to my father when they were around because it "brought everyone down." Ten years later, I was with my 20-year old daughter, sharing my sadness that my family insisted that I not have feelings at the time my father was dying. She reminded me, "You told us not to cry at the funeral. You said we would be upsetting Grandma if we did. I didn't like to have to hold back my tears because I was really sad."

I had forgotten that I had forced my children to keep their feelings hidden. Embarrassed that I had passed on the family teaching, I apologized to my daughter. That same week, I received a postcard from my mother who was trying to overcome some symptoms by seeing a hypnotist. She was annoyed with constant interruptions (phone calls, etc.) during her sessions, so she decided to stop the visits. She wanted to tell the therapist of her annoyance, but my step-father told her she was just indulging herself. She then told me not to mention this in any of my letters. She didn't want to discuss it. My hunch is that the family tradition of suppressing feelings contributed to the onset of her second bout of cancer, which eventually killed her.

Not only is depression an unnatural response to events, it generally creates more difficulties in a person's life. Withdrawal from one's daily life and relationships is a serious secondary loss. When the feelings associated with these added losses are suppressed, the result is greater energy loss, and the individual becomes enmeshed in a downward spiral. If something doesn't change, and the depression continues over time, it begins to take a toll on the body's immune system, which then cannot ward off illnesses. If illness ensues, the body is less able to heal itself, and the situation grows even more serious

The only way out of this downward spiral is through the feelings. The use of drugs, prescribed or not, may interfere with the acknowledgment and expression of feelings and may postpone the work to be done.

All too often, there is a social bind that locks the depressed person into the depressed state: the family and friends who sincerely want the individual to stop being depressed don't want to be confronted with the feelings of sadness, anger, and fear. If the depressed person cannot see the solution, it is imperative that family members or friends develop an understanding of what is happening, become able to tolerate the feelings, enable the depressed person to begin to acknowledge and express them, and take the time required to do all this. The following workbook section will provide some guidelines about how to begin to work your way out of depression by opening to the feelings.

THE WORKBOOK:
WORKING YOUR WAY
OUT OF DEPRESSION

Sometimes you may feel "down," or "out-of-sorts," or simply disinterested in your usual activities. Or you may be feeling whatever you mean by "depressed," or "out-of-control" without being able to identify clearly what it is that is troubling you. This section on sorting out is designed to make it possible for you to begin to focus on what it is that is contributing to your "down" feeling.

Follow the general instructions for use of the workbook as described in Chapter One: have your journal or some blank pieces of paper and a pencil available; take time to yourself; begin with a period of relaxed breathing to become centered and grounded; remember to personalize and be specific in your writing.

Now, let your mind wander among all the things that are affecting your life right now: events, feelings about events (past or present), another person's reaction to your feelings, etc. Let your thoughts move freely, without judgment. As you do this, start making a simple written list of anything that comes to mind that might be contributing to your feeling down. As it comes to mind, put it down on the list; catch yourself in any inner debate about whether a particular item belongs on the list and just put it on. If it doesn't belong, you can take it out later.

Your task right now is only to make a list of factors that might be contributing to your feeling down. No need to explain or elaborate; just write a key word or phrase on the list. Take time now to complete your list before going on.

SORTING OUT:

Things that contribute to my feeling "down."

When you have listed everything that comes readily to mind, go on to the next part. If you think of something else later, you can add it to one of your lists.

Next, on fresh pages, write down headings for new lists like this:

Loss/Sadness   Hurt/Anger   Guilt/Shame   Fear

Now, look back at your original "sorting out" list and reconsider each item. If an item seems to represent a loss to you, that is, if you experience some sadness or become tearful as you think about it, write it down on the **Loss/Sadness** list

If an item might make you feel angry or hurt (if only the least bit), write it down on the **Hurt/Anger** list.

If an item causes you to experience some guilt or shame, or, as you think about it, contributes to your saying to yourself, "I should (shouldn't) have said (or done) that," write it down on the **Guilt/Shame** list.

If an item causes you to experience some fear or to imagine dire consequences, write it down on the **Fear** list.

Continue until each item has been transferred to a new list. If you have trouble deciding where to put a particular item, put it on more than one list.

As you proceed, one list or another may have more items on it. That's OK; it will help you to know where the weight of your feeling is. You also may think of new items; just put these on the appropriate list.

The purpose of this sorting out is to clarify exactly how these events are affecting your life right now. This will allow you to begin to acknowledge the feelings you have about these events. It also will help you end any confusion you might feel about the source of the feelings.

NOTES

CHAPTER FOUR

Shock & Stress Response

Physiological shock roughly parallels emotional shock. If you've ever fallen and "knocked the wind out of yourself," you have a pretty good idea of what physiological shock is all about. You experience the impact, some dizziness and stinging/hurting, and a growing awareness that something important has occurred in your universe:

> An awareness that you need to take a breath;
> An attempt at taking a breath;
> A rushing realization that you can't take a breath;
> A second attempt to breathe accompanied by a little panic, and then a little bit of air squeaking past your seized-up larynx;
> Diminished panic;
> More studied concentration on the act of inspiration;
> More success;
> Less panic;
> A sense of relief begins to develop.

(After the shock wears off, your emotions become available for expression, and you can ask yourself, "What happened?" And later, "How did this happen?")

But, even in a relatively mild experience, emotions are deferred to the need for physiological survival. Our initial response to the news of some tragedy is a feeling of shock accompanied by a sense of disbelief, "Oh, no!, This can't be true!" And we often behave as if it is not really true.

In the event of the death of someone you are close to, the initial impact is quite like the physical experience of falling and having the wind knocked out of you. The tragedy is a threat to the survival of your universe as you know it, and your response is the same as it would be to any threat to your survival: you go into a physiological stress response. Your feelings are deferred to the need to take care of the details of life.

A THREAT TRIGGERS A STRESS RESPONSE

Stress has been talked about so much in the popular media that you might believe any stress is to be avoided. The external stressors in life are inevitable. Stress response is a natural and desired part of life's plan in which your body, at a very primitive level, gets prepared to fight for your survival. Whenever your lower brain receives signals that there is a threat to your existence, it forces a stress response that moves instantly through your body. Through increased muscle tension, blood pressure, heart rate, respiration rate, and blood sugar level, your body becomes prepared either to fight or run, a reaction as primitive as the reaction of a deer in the woods when it's startled. Of course, this is useful to your survival when you are in real danger. It enables you to react with a strength and endurance that you would otherwise believe impossible. It is the basis for those amazing stories we sometimes hear: a mother lifts a car so her child, trapped underneath, can be rescued; a person rescues several people from a burning building without a thought of personal danger.

WE'RE "PUT ON HOLD"

Another characteristic of the stress response, important in any consideration of grief, is that while your body is caught up in the response, your emotions may be deferred or "put on hold." If, when in real danger, you stopped to contemplate how horrifying the situation was, you might not survive. In modern life, this response is put to use as you handle the details of catastrophic loss. It is during this period that the individual seemingly floats along in blissful ignorance. There is often an eerie calmness as funeral arrangements are made, clothing chosen to wear, food ordered to serve. Comments are made about how well the survivors are "coping" with this tragedy when, in fact, they have not yet begun to experience the full implications of the event. To attempt to help a person in this state "face reality" is usually fruitless and unnecessary.

Soon, due either to exhaustion or the absence of anything that might stimulate a stress response, the emotions appropriate to the event will begin to arise. Grief will proceed if not interrupted.

Here is a very common example in which feelings are temporarily deferred: you respond to some emergency swiftly and seemingly without fear only to feel surprised by a rush of horror, sadness, rage, etc., after the danger is past. This actually is a healthy response in that the feelings quickly catch up with you. The feelings are acknowledged, then naturally subside, and there is no "delayed stress response" to trouble you later on.

However, if you were to continue in the stress response, more than likely your emotions simply would not be available. The greater the emotional shock, the greater the stress response. An example that could lead to difficulty is seen when a person endures some frightful, traumatic experience and has not yet allowed the feelings about the experience to catch up. The intense feelings, linked with images of the experience, may continue to be so frightening that the person keeps going into stress response again and again, and the feelings continue to be deferred. This repetitive process can be the source of interrupted grief and ongoing pain in your life and is the source of the post-traumatic stress disorders and stress-related illnesses that may be the plague of modern life. We believe that this repetitive process can best be understood if envisioned as a cyclical predicament.

POST-TRAUMATIC STRESS CYCLE

The "Post-Traumatic Stress Cycle" is the basis for the chronic or delayed reactions many people experience for many months, or even years, following a traumatic or catastrophic loss. The cycle works like this:

1) When involved in a traumatic event, the body goes into a stress response that serves our survival needs by heightening our ability either to "fight or run"; we do what we can to survive or save the people we care about.

2) While we are in stress response, feelings—the emotional responses we might have to such an event if it didn't threaten our survival—are suppressed; that is, we don't stop in the burning building to express how horrifying this is. If the event is too horrifying, disgusting, humiliating, or otherwise alien to us, the memories of the event and the feelings may be deeply forgotten and therefore harder to access. This is often referred to as "having amnesia for the event".

3) Social expectations and pressure encourage us to continue to suppress the emotions. We may do our best to keep the emotions from surfacing by putting more energy into suppressing them, often aided by drugs, alcohol, food, or workaholic activity. The continual expenditure of energy to keep the feelings down results in the "energy-less" state of depression.

4) There seem always to be constant reminders of the event, however. Some sound, a smell, a certain word or quality of voice, the anniversary of the event, a dream or "nightmare," a movie depicting similar events, familiar places, etc., will trigger the re-surfacing of our feelings and memories of the event. If our feelings and memories were deeply forgotten, the sudden upsurge of both may be very frightening because there had been no conscious awareness that anything of this sort had been experienced and also because we've been socially trained to view these kind of "flashbacks" as "crazy," or "psychotic".

5) This "double whammy"—the fear of the feelings arising and the intensity of the feelings about and memories of the original event—contributes to our feeling as if the original event were recurring. We go into stress response again, our feelings get suppressed, and the cycle continues.

Please see chart on page 37.

Original Traumatic Event (stressor)
(read clockwise)
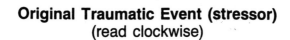

becomes
Stressor

Stress Response
(fight or run for survival;
emotions are suppressed)

As If Feeling

Fear of Feelings

Suppressed Emotions
(horror/fear,
rage/anger,
guilt/shame,
sadness,
embarrassment,
humiliation, etc.)

**Reawakening
of Feeling**

"Coping"
(continued suppression of feelings aided by too much alcohol/
drugs/food/work/etc.)

Something Stimulates Feelings
(fantasy of event,
nightmares,
familiar place,
anniversary of event,
familiar smells/sounds/words,
sleeplessness.)

Results In

Original Traumatic Event (stressor)
(read clockwise)

becomes
Stressor

Stress Response
(fight or run for survival;
emotions are suppressed)

As If Feeling

Fear of Feelings

**Reawakening
of Feeling**

Suppressed Emotions
(horror/fear,
rage/anger,
guilt/shame,
sadness,
embarrassment,
humiliation, etc.)

"Coping"
(continued suppression of feelings aided by too much alcohol/
drugs/food/work/etc.)

Something Stimulates Feelings
(fantasy of event,
nightmares,
familiar place,
anniversary of event,
familiar smells/sounds/words,
sleeplessness.)

Results In

AFTERMATH OF HOT-AIR BALLOON CRASH

The following is an example of a situation of catastrophic loss where the delayed stress cycle played a large part in interrupting the grieving process: (We appreciate David Favor and Judith Favor for allowing us to use this example.)

Peter: One sunny Saturday in December many years ago, some friends of mine who were hot-air balloon pilots and enthusiasts met with tragedy when their balloon failed to continue to rise after launch, was blown downwind about a quarter of a mile, and hit high-voltage power transmission lines. The balloon rose above the lines, the cables holding the gondola to the balloon shorted-out the power lines, and the resultant electrical arcing burned through the cables one by one, causing the gondola to tip precariously, then fall the sixty feet or so to the ground. My friend David and his passenger were thrown out of the gondola upon impact.

Judith, David's wife and flight instructor who had been handling the ground lines for this flight, ran after the balloon as she realized it was not rising and witnessed the fall of the gondola. She was at the scene almost immediately after the gondola crashed to the ground. Other witnesses called for medical assistance, and after some delays caused by communications difficulties, the two injured men were transported to a local hospital. The passenger was pronounced dead a few minutes after arrival, and David, unconscious, underwent surgery to repair extensive internal bleeding and his crushed pelvis and shattered leg. After five days in intensive care, David was out of danger, although in traction with a good deal of pain.

I was able to make the trip to visit the Saturday after the accident. I went directly to the hospital and found David to be heavily medicated but in good spirits considering his injuries and the outlook for an extended recovery period. He had amnesia for the accident, was sleeping fairly well, and had a fair amount of energy for visiting. Judith, on the other hand, was not sleeping;

her face was deeply lined, drained of color and painfully expressed her exhaustion. She could not talk about the accident without visibly trembling.

As I got ready to leave for the evening, I asked Judith, "Can I talk to you for a while? I'm worried that while David is the one who is physically injured, you seem to be the one who is suffering." She agreed to talk, and we spent the next four hours together, going over the details of the accident and her experience since then. I asked her to tell me exactly what she had been doing since the accident.

"Well, I made all the arrangements concerning David's hospitalization and his absence from work; I took care of getting accommodations for the people visiting; I've been caring for and talking to our children." (Two of them witnessed the accident.) "I haven't been able to sleep, even though the doctors have given me lots of medication. Whenever I start to fall to sleep, the scene of the balloon drifting downwind toward the power lines comes into my mind, and I wake up feeling as if the whole thing is happening all over again."

I shared my hunch with her: "I think what is happening has to do with the fact that you haven't yet expressed your feelings about the accident even though you've talked a lot about the details. As you fall asleep, the feelings begin to catch up with you, and they bring all of the associated images."

Judith agreed to allow the feelings to arise as we again went over the details, and I pressed her for her feelings about each detail. Indeed, her feelings were there, and she expressed her horror at the realization that the balloon was headed for the power lines, and her helplessness and guilt at not being able to intervene in what was happening. She was horrified as she saw the balloon rise above the power lines and the gondola catch the wires; she saw the balloon holding it there while the electrical arcing cut the cables. She expressed more horror as she described the gondola finally falling, with her husband and the passenger being thrown out. She was outraged not only at the communication difficulty that resulted in medical help being delayed but

She began to focus on her concern that when she went to administer what first-aid she could, David, being unconscious, seemed to be more in need than the passenger. The passenger groaned, and she took that to mean he was all right. With deep sadness and tears, she said, "I'm afraid that I could have done something that could have prevented his death, and I didn't do it!"

I asked her whether she knew what had caused his death. She said, "Yes, the doctor said it was a ruptured aorta." I asked her if she knew what that meant. She didn't. I told her about the aorta and its function and my belief that he could have fallen (from the balloon) into the emergency room at the best hospital in the world, and it would be unlikely that he could survive such a serious injury.

With that information, Judith's tears flooded her being. She cried with deep, wrenching sobs for a long time, and when she stopped, the furrowed, tight lines in her face had smoothed out as she finally seemed relieved of the pain. She described feeling truly tired, so we parted.

When I saw her the next day, she said she had not taken any medication and had slept well for the first time since the accident. We said goodbye, and I left feeling as though she had been able to release some of her grief successfully.

THE WORKBOOK:
FEELINGS OF
SHOCK & STRESS RESPONSE

Begin as directed earlier by seeking out a place where you can be uninterrupted. Take a few minutes to sit in a relaxed breathing position and do some deep breathing in order to become more relaxed and focused on the work at hand. Then, on a fresh page write the heading:

Stress Response

Write down any of the feelings you identified earlier as belonging to "stressfulness" and any feelings you would identify with being in a "state of shock."

Now, take a minute or two to recall the last time you narrowly missed having an accident—on the highway, skiing, boating—then write down your recollections of the incident. After you've finished, read back over what you've written and insert any description of feelings you may have left out. Describing your feelings about a past incident in this way will very likely bring up current feelings. If so, take a few minutes to experience these as fully as you can. Then, write a description of what you are experiencing.

When you are through writing, return to the relaxed breathing position and concentrate on slowing your breathing down and breathing very deeply. If it is hard for you to resume slow, deep breathing, imagine that there is a lighted candle across the room from you and blow at it hard enough to move a lot of air and get the flame to flicker. Your next inspiration will be deeper, and it will be easier to slow down from there.

Next, take a few minutes to recall when you first learned about the primary loss you are working on now. Then take all the time you need to write down your recollections, including what you experienced as bodily sensations/feelings at the time you heard about what happened.

Again, you will experience some feelings in the present.

As you become aware of the feelings, describe these as well. If you feel uncomfortable with the feelings, take your relaxed breathing position and resume slow, deep breathing as above. As you become comfortable again, write down a description of the uncomfortable feelings.

Notice that if the feelings have anything to do with being afraid, scared, panicked, stressed, anxious, etc., they begin to resolve as you resume deep, slow breathing. This is similar to "heaving a sigh of relief" after the danger has passed. Your stress response is characterized by a general quickening of breathing and heart rate, which you may notice along with the tightening of your back, neck, and stomach muscles. As you reverse your breathing rhythm to slow and deep, your body gets the signal to "slow down", and a general relaxation will follow.

NOTES

CHAPTER FIVE

Sadness & Anger

Nature provides for the stress response to diminish after the threat has passed. The physiological stress response begins to wear off as physical exhaustion sets in. Awareness expands to encompass the external world enough to begin to grasp the reality of what has happened and even later to consider the event's full implications. It is this rising awareness that a profound tragedy has occurred that is the opening to grief.

Sadness is the "gut" experience of loss and perhaps the emotion most commonly expected in our grief. It is that sinking feeling of dismay we experience when we believe that we've lost something of value. Consider a very simple example:

> You are tired and it's pouring down rain. You are walking toward your car after an extra-long day at work required to finish an overdue project. As you near your car, you reach for the place where you usually keep your car keys and find—nothing. Your heart sinks into your belly as you stop short and search again, incredulous that your keys are not there. You are momentarily stunned by the impact of this sudden change in your world. Not believing, you look again, and as it becomes apparent to you that the keys are not there, you are momentarily seized by an unexpected sense of fear. The words, "What am I going to do?" race through your brain before your

lips can shape their sounds. At the same time, your survival instinct has begun to search through all the possibilities of where the keys could be. "It's unthinkable that they could be lost! They must be here somewhere." With a sudden realization, you remember that you wore a different jacket than usual and put the keys in one of the pockets, and, "Yes, here they are!" You pull the keys out and open your car door and, with a sigh of relief, sit down and insert the key into the ignition. You let the sound of the engine starting bring your stress level down to something manageable enough for you to drive home.

This experience ends without a loss and, as such, does not flow into the emotions that would follow a real loss. It does, however, lend some insight into that "sinking feeling" that accompanies a real loss and eventually becomes the deep sadness that is associated with profound loss.

LOSS, SADNESS, AND TEARS

Tears are the outward sign that you are experiencing a sense of loss. If you are filling with tears, look for some loss behind the veil of tears. ("Is there anything about this that may imply a loss?") As you look more deeply into the possibilities, you almost always connect with some specific loss. The simple act of acknowledging that the tears imply something not yet understood, or not yet in full awareness, opens you to uncover what is beneath the tears.

Let's say that you are crying as you watch a movie about a child who lost his mother. You explore your tears and find you are missing your own mother even though you thought you were done grieving her death. As the specifics of your loss are brought into focus, you come to know clearly what you miss about your mother and the role she played in your life. As you come to know these things, you also come to know what you cared about the most and what memories you want to preserve.

Acknowledging sadness, then, can bring into focus what you cared about, how much you cared, and, in so doing, helps to diminish the possibility of secondary losses occurring.

SECONDARY LOSSES

Peter: A community-based organization asked me, as a last resort, to see a woman, "B", who seemed quite depressed and whom the counselors could not seem to "get a handle on." When I asked B what was going on, she referred back about twenty years and described a hard-fought battle with a progressively disabling illness. She was currently unable to manage her life without attendant care, but, if she had the help, she thought she would be doing all right. I decided to ask B if there wasn't something else that was contributing to her feeling so "down" right now; she dissolved into tears and, after a few minutes, was able to say, "My mother just died." With this as the focus, we were then able to get to the depth of her sadness and begin to work out of it with a clear idea of what was going on. B's ninety-year-old mother had been physically strong and vigorous but was deteriorating intellectually. She had been able to provide the physical care her daughter needed, and B was able to manage their affairs even though she was physically incapacitated. Their perfect "teamwork" was destroyed by the mother's sudden death from a heart attack. While B had been able to pull together the resources to manage her physical needs, she had been unable to connect with the profound sadness she was experiencing about the loss of her primary friend and confidante. Because of this, a serious secondary loss occurred: she was isolating herself because she had been unable to respond to letters from friends and relatives and reveal that her mother had died. Several sessions were needed to work through her sadness; her depression resolved, and she was able to resume her correspondence and involvement with friends and relatives.

Note: The counselors at this agency had been focusing on the woman's disability rather than her feelings regarding her losses. The disability was really not the issue, and the focus on it only encouraged this person to talk less about what was really going on.

ANGER

Anger is a response to some hurt. Our primitive instinct to react to hurt by feeling angry operates just the same today as it did millions of years ago. The simplest example of the hurt/anger reaction is that of hitting your finger with a hammer:

> At practically one and the same time, you recoil from the blow, throw the hammer down, and yell some very forceful and unkind remarks about the hammer, the nail, and life in general. Perhaps it occurs to you that it's unfair that this happened to you, and you may decide to give up your attempts at building. But, after a short while, you take up the hammer again with the resolve to do your best not to repeat the hurtful act.

Very simple, really: a hurt, an expression of anger, and, after a time, a return to life. We believe that the only difference between this and the reaction to a profound hurt such as a death is that the anger is profound. Remember that the more you care about someone, the more you will feel hurt if you lose that person. This is pure and simple personal outrage at the fact of being hurt. "Why me?" "Why did our son have to die? What purpose could this serve?" For any person to lose a loved one, to become seriously ill, to become injured, is, for that person, an outrage. This rage is "pure" in that it really has no object, i.e., a person at whom one is angry. It is anger at the hurt at having the roots of your life-as-you-know-it torn out of your soul, at having an irreplaceable gap in your universe. Now, what exactly is the value of recognizing and expressing this anger?

There are two basic results: first, it will help you avoid becoming depressed, and, if it accomplishes nothing else, this will have value because becoming depressed can only compound your losses. Second, it will help you identify what specifically is hurtful about this loss. As you identify what hurts you, you also are identifying those things that you care most about.

This can include preserving your fond memories of the person you've lost. Too often, friends or family members may suggest that it's too painful to remember what the lost person meant to you; they may say you are "wallowing in self-pity." If you are angry that anyone wants to take your memories away, you can use that anger/energy release to be assertive in telling people that you intend to keep talking about and remembering the things you cared for in your loved one.

Now, we are not talking about a popular notion. There is not much encouragement to express anger, and there are few models showing us how to express anger in a constructive or non-hurtful way. Many of us have been led to believe that if we are legitimately to verbalize our anger, we must focus on someone who has wronged us or something that has hurt us. But what if there is no one to blame? To add to the dilemma, if we do express our outrage, we run the risk that anyone within earshot may presume that we are angry at them, and they quickly remind us that we have no business being so. Some anger may be acknowledged as legitimate where there is a negligent party involved. But for those who can find no one at fault, the societal expectation to suppress feelings may interfere with the verbalization of the anger.

There is an important interplay between sadness and anger that can be upset if anger is not openly acknowledged. This has to do with the balance that can be achieved where the "down" experience of sadness and the "up" experience of anger are both expressed. Both are powerful emotions, but anger is the more energizing of the two. If the "down" experience of sadness is expressed, but the energizing effect of the anger must be suppressed, there is no balance. This creates a higher likelihood of the grieving person's slipping toward depression, which we believe is a state to be avoided at all costs. (See Chapter Three)

Many people don't want to experience anger because they have confused the feeling of anger with the acting-out of that anger. Reminded of angry actions that may have had hurtful results, most people back away from the feeling entirely.

Let's assume that you have some awareness of your anger. Here are some choices and possible results:

1) Push the anger (energy) down so that it isn't appar-

ent. This results in depression, a very destructive state in which the anger may be directed at one's self.

2) Fight. This is the most troublesome choice, obviously, because of the possibility of inflicting hurt.

3) Run away. This avoids the issue but may feel safer at the time. Unfortunately, the problem runs with you.

4) Be physically active—jogging, wood cutting, exercise. This does use up some energy, but it does not focus on the real issue, and it does nothing to prevent the anger from returning in full force.

5) Verbal expression. It may be surprising, but there is enough expression in your words and the energy behind them to acknowledge and dissipate the force of the anger you feel.

You must choose a safe environment in which to express your anger. The person(s) with whom you express your feelings may be a family member or a friend. If necessary, you might choose a counselor who has experience in working effectively with anger. The purpose s/he serves is to encourage you to verbalize all the anger you are feeling without taking the anger personally. Some of the anger may go back to other hurtful experiences around which you never expressed how you felt. This expression serves to "update" your anger. The angry feelings must be expressed in such a way as to focus them into very specific terms. The workbook can guide you through this. It is sometimes useful to combine physical activity with direct focus on the angry feelings. Going to the dump with a lot of old jars, broken dishes, etc., and hurling glass so that you hear the crash and feel the power in your arm may release more feelings. You actually will experience the energy in your body and the strength behind that energy. As long as there is continual re-focusing on what your rage is about, you will release the anger safely, and the energy it took to hold it down will be available to you. You will feel lighter and better able to deal with life decisions and your relationships.

THE WORKBOOK:
CLARIFYING YOUR SADNESS & ANGER

Again, sit comfortably and breathe deeply and get ready to work on loss/sadness and hurt/anger. You will be specifying even the most minute, often forgotten, or embarrassing feelings.

On a fresh page of your journal, write the heading:

Loss/Sadness

Write down the bodily sensations you have when you think about your primary loss or feel sad for any reason.

Write down any other names you have for these feelings. Next, take your primary loss, and write about it in the following manner:

(primary loss)   (secondary loss)

As a result of (my loss), I also have lost _____

As a result of (my loss), I also have lost _____

As a result of (my loss), I also have lost _____

Continue until you are unable to think of any other way that the event represents a loss to you.

It is important for you to maintain the above structure in order to avoid intellectualizing or generalizing. Remember, your experience is unique to you. The structure will help you know specifically what the loss is about.

Example:

1) As a result of my son's death, I have lost seeing all the kids that used to come play with him.

2) As a result of my son's death, I have lost my dream of being able to share my interests with my only son.

3) As a result of my son's death, I have lost the possibility

of having a closer relationship with my son than I was able to have with my father.

    4) As a result of my son's death, I have lost...

    Notice that you have created a list of your secondary losses; you now can proceed by selecting a secondary loss to work with and continue as above, using the following as an example:

    1) As a result of my loss of not being able to share my interests with my only son, I have lost my enthusiasm for sailing.

    2) As a result of my loss of not being able to share my interests with my only son, I have lost my desire to go fishing.

    3) As a result of my loss of not being able to share my interests with my only son, I have lost my love for kite-flying.

    4) And so on...

    Another example beginning with the primary loss:

    1) As a result of the death of my husband, I am sad that I have lost a close companion.

    2) As a result of the death of my husband, I am sad that I have lost a person I could talk to about anything.

    3) As a result of the death of my husband, I am sad that I have lost a person I could talk to about everything.

    4) As a result of the death of my husband, I am sad that I have lost a source of income.

    5) As a result of the death of my husband, I am sad that I have lost my ability to pay the taxes on our home.

    6) And so on...

In this example, you can see the list of secondary losses that has emerged. Each one of them deserves exploration. Items (4) and (5), for example, represent significant losses and suggest further consequences that must be acknowledged so that appropriate decisions about them can be made. (You also may discover some anger, guilt, fear, or shame that results from your closer examination of some of these secondary losses. If so, it is important that you add them to the appropriate lists.)

After you've written all you can think of for now in the loss/sadness section, take a few minutes again to sit comfortably and do some deep breathing.

On another fresh page in your journal write the heading:

Hurt/Anger

Write down the bodily sensations you have when you're feeling hurt or angry.

Write down any other names you have for these feelings.

Next, select a single item from your anger list and then write down everything that might contribute to your feeling hurt or angry about that (however "trivial or petty" that might be). Include even the most minor annoyances and acknowledge that they all add up to a large feeling of anger. Now that you have experience with the process, you may shorten your sentences:

Because my only son died of AIDS,
1) I feel angry that research hasn't turned up a cure.
2) I feel angry that he was so young.
3) I feel angry that the government took so long to endorse education about AIDS.
4) I feel angry that he will be judged because of his illness.

Now, (3) might bring a focus on feeling angry about attitudes and moral judgments, and these can be worked through in the same fashion. For example:

Because the government's moral judgments delayed funding for education,
1) I feel angry that others also will die because of a lack of education.
2) I feel angry that we don't have a representative government.

In addition, these are further revelations of secondary losses that can be acknowledged in the same fashion as in the "Loss/Sadness" section.

Go ahead now with your list. Keep to the task of personalizing and being specific as you work. As you realize additional items of loss, anger, etc., add them to the appropriate list and work these through as well.

NOTES

CHAPTER SIX

Guilt & Shame

A sense of guilt may be one of the primary obstacles to a resolution of the feelings associated with loss because guilt interferes with even beginning to sort out or work through all the other feelings. If you are not moving through your grief, then you may feel as though life must teach you a lesson: that is, you need to be punished. In this event, you may be carrying/feeling shame. There is a difference between experiencing guilt and experiencing shame, and we will separate these as clearly as we can.

GUILT
The basic idea of guilt is: it is the price you pay when your behavior violates some standard or belief you hold. As long as your behavior is violating the standard, guilt will follow. Very often, the standard is not very clear in your consciousness, and you begin to question your behavior only in response to a feeling of guilt or shame.

Guilt seems to have its origins in the "magical thinking" of early childhood: the child's belief in his/her own power, growing out of the reality that the newborn child is the "center of the universe." The child learns that when s/he has a need (for clean diapers, food, etc.), all the child has to do is make a sound, and someone comes to fill the need. This belief continues until the child's intellectual level (age six to nine) allows him/her to start understanding other cause and effect relationships in the world. Parenting figures can be instrumental in helping children understand that they are not re-sponsible for everything that happens, and generally we reach maturity with a sense of responsibility that does not un-dermine our sense of worth.

Even the most effectively functioning families differ in their approaches to life, and some of us may lock-in a certain remnant of magical thinking. Perhaps we were "imprinted" with a suggestion that stuck: "You'll be the death of me yet." (If we believed this, and the person died, we would retain the belief that we caused the death.) Some family "sub-cultures" teach that to expect anything good will only bring bad, and vice versa. So, if you were thinking that the person would live, and they died, then you would assume that your positive thinking created something bad. Even under the best of cir-cumstances, we adults retain a bit of magical thinking that contributes to a sense of guilt in response to any profound loss. "What did I do to cause this?" "What could I have done to prevent this?" These are perfectly reasonable questions for adults to be asking about their effect on the world, and it is natural that they would arise around the loss. Whether or not they linger to torment us may depend upon the degree of "magical thinking" we retain from our childhood.

SHAME

When a person feels shamed easily, we can think of this as an extreme form of guilt that includes a profound loss of self-esteem. The person (more than likely) comes from a fam-ily that allowed the child to take responsibility for how things went and that encouraged the child to feel overly responsible through blaming and finding fault whenever things went wrong. This super-responsibility may be seen as an asset as the child grows toward maturity, but throughout life even a trivial infraction noticed by some authority figure (parents, teachers, employers, etc.) can instill a sense of personal fail-ure and further diminish self-worth. Therefore, whenever behavior violates a standard, the person immediately sinks to a very low state, in which he/she feels worthless.

A STORY FROM CHILDHOOD

Zeva: When I was about five (not reading yet and not

able to write letters, words), I made a decision. I wanted the neighbors to come to my house and help my father stop screaming in his sleep. I carefully took pencil, paper, and envelopes and composed "scribble" letters to all the neighbors. I stuffed the envelopes and wrote "scribble" addresses on the outside of each envelope. I then delivered all the "letters" to the mailboxes on our street. When my mother found out (I suppose the neighbors saw me and spoke with her), she frightened me with her anger. She yelled and screamed and threatened me, calling me awful names. I felt shamed and ridiculed, and I vowed never again to write anything important that others could read.

A sense of shame followed me into adulthood. Here are a few examples of how it has affected me: I used to cringe every time I was interviewed for a newspaper article; I was sure I would say "the wrong thing" and be punished severely. I apologized profusely to my children for the terrible job I did as a parent; I could see all my errors, and my shame prefaced all conversations about our past. One day, my nineteen-year-old daughter said to me: "Mom, how long are you going to feel guilty and ashamed of those days? It really interferes with being with you now. You never talk about the good things, the good times. You were really a wonderful mom in many ways even though there were some awful times." My tears were hot as they flooded my eyes and spilled down my face. She was right; I was afraid to say that I did the best I could. I had some kind of "addiction" to holding on to the suffering. I was ashamed of how I acted at times with my children; that was true, and it also was true that I no longer did hurtful things to them. I had learned something, and I used my guilt about what I had done to change my behavior. Guilt can be a way for your conscience to speak to you. It says, "Don't do that again," and that is healthy.

Sometimes I look back with humor at my acute sense of responsibility and concern that I would do something wrong. Peter was very confused by this when we were first together. If his car wasn't running, I took it as my responsibility and, without his agreement, took over any tasks that he might have planned. I second-guessed him all the time because I didn't want him to be angry with me. After several years of this, he said, "What do I have to do to let you know that I don't get angry with you over these things? If I am angry with you, I will tell you directly." It took me years to believe him. I was sure that he would catch me in a shameful act, and he would be very angry. My behavior has changed quite a bit since then because I have found the roots of my shame in my family-of-origin's dysfunctional patterns. The only way I could break the pattern was to confront the damage my parents had done, stop idealizing them, get my own history straight, and look for the suppressed anger that lay behind the shame. Once that was acknowledged, I could see my parents more realistically, and slowly my chronic guilt and co-dependent behavior diminished.

People often ruminate about how they could have made a difference "if only they had . . ." The fact is that we do what we do at the time because that is all that we know how to do. History may show that what happened did not have a good ending, but it is unfair to use hindsight to judge your previous decisions. Using the Acknowledgment Approach, you can examine everything you did, the result of your action, and what you feel about that result. When guilt comes in after the event, you must look for the standard you hold for your behavior that expects you to do more than you knew how to do, or were capable of, at the time. Chronic guilt, carried shame, endless ruminating will result in depression.

SENSE OF FAILURE
When people feel personally responsible for something that is out of their control, they may experience a sense of personal failure if there is an undesirable outcome. This can be seen in the "survivor's guilt" of combat veterans and others who survive a catastrophic event in which a friend or family member has died or been injured. Health professionals are also vulnerable in this situation, especially those in long-term care if they come to care deeply for their patients and clients. Very often, the standard held out to health care providers is to preserve or maintain life. So what happens when a care provider does everything s/he can to help someone, and the person dies anyway? There is lots of feeling and an abun-

dance of guilt. The strict adherence to the standard can produce a sense of failure and depression if the extreme guilt is allowed to interrupt the grieving. Of course, if the guilt is allowed to surface, the other feelings will begin to move also, and all will be available to be acknowledged openly and explored in detail.

The following example can serve to demonstrate what we mean.

HOSPITAL STAFF RESPONDS TO LOSS

Peter: I was asked to consult with a hospital staff responsible for the care of children who had been diagnosed at an early age as having a serious progressive illness. Through daily treatments, the staff was able to help the young people lead relatively active lives. Because of the inevitable advancement of the disease process, however, life expectancy did not extend beyond late teen years. The request for the consultation was based on concern over the fact that individual staff members had responded intensely to the recent death of one of the young people who had been in their care. However, their grief was directed inwardly and was expressed as depression or discouragement, and one staff member had been hospitalized with a perforated ulcer following the child's death. I met with the group of physicians, physical therapists, respiratory therapists, nurses, and others weekly for nearly a year. As my involvement began to be trusted, and people discussed their feelings more openly, I began to understand that from the intensive work and continued involvement with the young people, the staff felt emotionally close to them, some to the degree that they were even reluctant to take vacations. They developed a strong sense of personal responsibility for the preservation of the child's life, and when the child began to lose ground in that battle, the staff experienced it as a personal failure, taking the blame for the child's death upon their own shoulders.

As the consultation progressed, the staff began to realize their dilemma: if they were involved with a child who had this illness, then they were involved with a child who had a high probability of an early death, and if they were going to perceive the child's death as a personal failure, then they were bound to fail. As they began to confront the cruelty of their dilemma, and openly expressed their frustration and anger, they stopped interrupting their own grieving process. They then could move toward an acknowledgment of their direct contribution to an extension of the child's life, a contribution that increased the child's involvement with family, friends, and community. The staff also realized that their sense of personal failure had interfered with their involvement with the child and parents as the child's death was anticipated. They in effect "lost" the child long before the child's actual death. As they continued to discuss their situation and all their feelings about it, their perception of a child's death began to shift from one of personal failure to that of personal loss.

The grieving process stopped being interrupted; it was acknowledged and honored instead of ignored, displaced, or "stuffed." This new awareness was put to the test near the end of the consultation when a 16-year-old was nearing death. In contrast to the earlier approach, the staff was able to continue to be involved with the child and parents in a close, personal way, including their acknowledgment with the child that she was approaching death, and that they were experiencing sorrow and loss about that. The parents were invited to stay at the hospital, not only to be more closely involved with their child, but to make decisions about her treatment in conjunction with the physician, who canceled his office appointments away from the hospital in order to be more available to them

Following the child's death, the staff openly expressed their feelings of sadness, anger, and frustration, but there were no resultant depressions and no hospitalizations for physical illness in response to emotional stress.

THE WORKBOOK:
CLARIFYING YOUR GUILT

Remember to do some relaxed breathing and let your breath ground you before you begin the work on your list. You are choosing items that stimulate feelings of guilt. Transfer the first item to a separate sheet of paper. Then, following the item, write down your action or behavior, the event that followed your action, and your "hindsight" regarding the proper standard. (The fact that you feel guilty implies that you hold some standard you have not been able to meet.)

ITEM: I feel guilty about not having done enough to help my friend who was sick.

Action or behavior	Event that followed	Standard
I put all my efforts into nursing my friend back to health.	My friend died.	Responsible nursing assures recovery.

In order to work through a feeling of guilt, it is necessary to examine your standard (or belief) as it conflicts with your behavior. Unless one or the other is changed so that they are consistent, you will have a resulting feeling of guilt. If you have some fears about changing the standard or behavior, you can weigh out the pros and cons, using the example shown in Chapter Seven.

Continue with each item until you have worked through your list. As with fears, it is important to acknowledge any sense of guilt that remains unresolved as some of the feeling affecting your life. As we said earlier in this chapter, it is useful to examine closely the decisions you made with which you are now finding fault. Here is another example using the format:

ITEM: I feel guilty about wrecking my car.

Action or behavior	Event that followed	Standard
I drove 65 mph.	I had an accident & wrecked my car.	Drive at the speed limit.

Why was I driving fast? I was lost in thought. Why was I lost in thought? Too many things were happening in my life that I didn't understand, and they were all chasing around in my head. Did I have a way to let those things go and focus on my driving? No. Did I plan on having an accident? No. Have I learned how to focus on my driving now? Yes. Do I need to hold on to the guilt now because I think I need to be punished? Maybe. Will it make my life worse if I keep feeling guilty? Yes. Will it keep me from being close to people? Yes. Do I want that? No. (Use your journal to record dialogue like this.) Chronic guilt has an addictive force to it. A little guilt can be a help to your conscience. Distinguishing chronic guilt or shame from intermittent guilt will be helpful.

If you do the exercises in this part and you don't experience a diminution of your guilt, you may be carrying shame from your childhood. Go to the chapter on children and complete your lifeline as well as you can. Look for those incidents in which you felt shame, then look for the hurt and anger that underlies any experience of shame. It was outrageous for you to have been shamed as a child. Normal, caring, functional parents will talk to their children when the children have done something that is outside of the boundaries of the family rules. They will talk with compassion and caring, not with shaming words, threats, or abuse. Your hurt/anger about your childhood can be identified and worked through by using the workbook for Chapter Five.

If your work on this stimulates any additional feelings of loss, anger, or fear, place these on the appropriate list and work through in turn.

NOTES

CHAPTER SEVEN

Fear

The working through of the fears that have been generated by a loss may be the most powerful and effective tool for getting prepared to "go on with life." Fear also can be the "Great Interrupter" of grief if our fear of intense feeling causes us to go into a stress response so that the feelings are deferred, suppressed, and delayed. We can allow the feelings to come up, especially the fears, when we begin to understand that the feelings are not the enemy; they are not the danger. The feelings can help us discover where we are in relation to a loss. Opening to the fear, in particular, can help us to know where we need to use caution in our lives. And it will help us recognize where we are safe, capable, and secure in our ability to survive the dangers we have been worried about.

VULNERABILITY

Most of us proceed with our lives as if we were omnipotent. That is, we don't usually imagine that we can be hurt in any way. For example, we hear statistics about auto accidents, and we know the laws and warnings to use seat belts: 65,000 people a year are killed in auto accidents, and more than 1,000,000 are permanently disabled. But unless an accident has touched us personally, we continue to drive without using seat belts/ shoulder harnesses, believing it's only "other" people who get hurt. When we do get touched by some tragic loss, it shatters our sense of omnipotence, and we are left with an exquisite sense of vulnerability. Once you have been hurt, you know you can be hurt. And if once, why not again? Or if this, why not that? And what if...and what if...and what if... keeps coming up again and again.

If you've been in a car accident, you will feel a bit shaky and be a little more cautious when you decide to drive again; if you are injured in a car accident, you'll be even more cautious; if you've been injured and cannot fully recover, i.e., have become "disabled," you'll feel even more vulnerable to further hurt. If you have had a relationship break up, you will worry about whether a new relationship can last. If you have developed a serious illness, you will tend to re-evaluate everything that relates to your health and your life. If you have lost a child, you will fear for your other children. If someone you care for dies, you will fear for the others you care for, including yourself.

To sustain a significant loss in your life essentially destroys your experiential base for managing your life, and without an experiential base, you can have no confidence about how your life will proceed. This very often leads you to re-evaluate your life in all ways: "Is this what I want to be doing?" "Is it worthwhile?" "Is it safe?"

To begin to work out of this period of uncertainty, it is necessary to consider, in detail, all the bits of worry or fear you may have. If you're worried about your health, be specific about what aspect of your health you are worried about. Are you:

gaining weight?	dull?
losing weight?	pressure? deep?
gaining strength?	when does it come?
losing strength?	when does it go?
gaining endurance?	does it move around?
losing endurance?	do you have any lumps or masses?
feeling pain?	where?
where?	what else can you tell me?
what does it feel like?	and so on...
sharp?	

With practice, you will become able to be just as specific

about any aspect of your life. As you begin to deeply explore the fears you have, you will come to know most completely how this loss has wounded you:

It is this wide, and this deep.
This part of me will not recover.
These parts of me are still intact.
This is where I need most to focus my energy.

Too often, the fears don't have a chance to present themselves when a person is preoccupied with his/her sense of loss and anger. But now that you've had a chance to work through some of your sadness, anger, and guilt, you are ready to start on your fears.

THE WORKBOOK:
WORKING THROUGH FEARS

You may be aware of some fear that you are ready to work on now. Whatever the fear is, the task of working it through begins in the same way as the work on loss, anger, and guilt.

Take a few minutes to do some breathing, get relaxed and focused.

On a fresh page of your journal, write the heading:

Vulnerability/Fear

Write down the bodily sensations that you have when you are feeling vulnerable or afraid.

Write down any other names you have for these feelings.

Next, write down a list of fears or add to any fears you might already have on your list. You may have a fear of this process, fears generated by the primary loss you are working on, something from a previous loss, or fears from any source; the process works well with any fear.

On a fresh piece of paper, take the first item from your list and start with the worst possible thing you think might happen, then the next worst, etc. Remember to be as specific as you possibly can be.

Then write down at least one way that you can avoid or prevent that particular thing from occurring. Do that for each item on your list. If you encounter an item for which you can think of no prevention at the moment, leave some clear, blank space below it, then move on to the next item.

Example:
1) I am afraid to let my other child out of my sight.
2) The worst possible thing that could happen as a result of letting her out of my sight would be that she might die like her sister did.
3) The next worst possible thing that could happen would be that the more I try to control her, the more reckless she becomes, and the more frightened I become. . . .

How can I prevent the worst possible thing from happening?

1) I can "let go," and hope that she doesn't have a terrible accident; I don't know if I can do that!

You can see that, as you continue, you may encounter an item for which the prevention leads to other fears. As these present themselves, add them to the list and take them up in turn. (You may also encounter things that need to be added to other lists.)

Example:
1) I am afraid to let my child make her own choices about what to risk.

In this case, use the following questions to weigh the pros and cons of the situation:

What do I stand to gain if I allow my child to risk?
What do I stand to lose if I allow my child to risk?
What do I stand to gain if I don't allow my child to risk?
What do I stand to lose if I don't allow my child to risk?

After you have gone completely through your list of fears, look back over it and reconsider any items for which you could think of no prevention. If you still feel concerned about these items and still can't think of any prevention, put them down on a separate page as a way to separate out the items for which you have no solution.

Fears for which I do not yet have a solution.

1) _____

2) _____

3) _____

Etc. _____

It is as important to acknowledge that there are some things about which you are afraid and for which you have no preventions at the present time as it is to acknowledge that there are fears that you can prevent.

NOTES

CHAPTER EIGHT

Talking with Children about Loss

You were born without any pre-conceived notions about the universe you were entering; it just was whatever it was for you. Your mother's voice, her general level of tension or relaxation, and her health directly affected you before birth. You may have been soothed by your familiarity with your mother in the otherwise unfamiliar environment outside her womb.

EARLY CHILDHOOD AWARENESS OF THE WORLD

In your early years, you spent most of your time learning about your universe, the people and things in it, what happened when you made certain noises, what it meant when your caretakers made certain noises. Whatever presented itself simply was taken as another part of what the world was like. Life for you from about one to four or five was like an elevator ride:

When the door opened, you saw a picture of the world.
When the door closed, your tummy tickled.
The door opened, and the world had changed.
The door closed; your tummy tickled.
The door opened, and the world had changed again.
And so on, and so on.

Young children are checking out their world every waking moment, taking for granted that every new experience is to be embraced and investigated. They'll check things out with every faculty at their command. If they can see, they'll look; if they can hear, they'll listen. They will do their best to get close to whatever they are investigating. They'll try to touch it, smell it, taste it, feel it against their body. They'll do all this with interest and vigor—unless they get hurt by it. If they're hurt by something they're investigating, their first response is to be startled and bewildered. Then they may cry, display some outrage, and try to get away from the offending object. Children who have begun to use language will use some words that will express their sadness or anger. Here's an example:

> A four-year-old child playing in a creek with Zeva was aware that his feet were getting wet. He looked agitated. She asked him, "Isn't that OK?" "No," he said, "my mom gets really mad at me when I get them wet." "Then what happens to you?" Zeva asked. "I get sad, and then I get mad, too. And then I jump and jump on my bed. Then I need a hug."

This child is broadening his perspective, and this can begin at a surprisingly early age, depending upon a particular child's intellectual development.

Children will learn their responses either through direct experience, or by following their parenting person's modeling of "the way to react to this thing." (Chapter Two.)

Zeva has a behavior, modeled after her mother, that has been difficult for Peter at times. It is a kind of "startle response," a quick gasp of air with sound. It is especially annoying when driving because it tends to startle the driver without giving any information. Zeva's mother did this whenever she became afraid. It was impossible not to incorporate the behavior, and it is nearly impossible to get rid of it.

The child in the environment of the parenting figure will model the presenting behavior, language patterns, intonation, style, etc., no matter what the parent wants. ("Do as I say, not as I do," is impossible.) As a young parent, Zeva remembers being horrified when she heard her three-year-old daughter telling a friend off with the same voice patterns that Zeva used when angry with her children.

Language learning is thought to be a result of an intrinsic

mechanism, coded genetically, that is ready to be used as soon as a child hears language (specifically phonemes) spoken. That mechanism allows a child not only to reproduce language heard, but also to make up new words as well as putting words together into sentences that are original. Peter's daughter, Jennifer, created words like "re-membory" (a combination of "memory" and "remember"), and "You'll be exciting" (for "You'll be excited about how interesting this is").

When she was three and a half or four, Jennifer invented a very clever phrase. It was at a community pot-luck dinner where there were lots of other parents, some with disabilities, some without. She asked, "Can standing mans be 'daddies' too?" Now, she had been exposed to other Daddies who were standing mans, but in her world, Daddy used a wheelchair, so she hadn't put together before this that standing-mans maybe could be daddies too.

ACKNOWLEDGING CHILDREN'S LOSSES

Small children will talk to you as best they can about any subject as long as you are encouraging. It is helpful, of course, to have a way to relate a new experience to something they already know about, and we usually do that with confidence.

Whether or not we are comfortable talking to children about loss, however, will depend upon whether we are up-to-date with our own grief. And that will depend upon whether:

(1) our role models were able to speak to us about personal losses—theirs and ours—and/or
(2) we took it upon ourselves to work on our own losses through therapy, etc.

If a child's lesser losses are acknowledged and the feelings are explored to the extent the child is interested, the child will gradually develop a base of experience from which to understand the impact of greater losses, up to and including the death of someone they love.

Sometimes someone dies, and people think that young children are too young to know the facts, so they are not told, even if it is their mother or father, sister or brother, grandmother or grandfather, or some special person that has cared for them.

If the person's life/death is not spoken of, children learn not to ask about it. If they don't get any information, the truth will remain shrouded in mystery, and they will be uneasy about the way "something" seems to be happening while everyone is pretending it "isn't happening."

Peter remembers hearing about his mother's death when he was ten. It is an example of, "It isn't significant."

> **Peter:** My parents were separated when I was very young. For fairly complicated reasons, my custody was vested in my father, who remarried when I was about six years old. We lived in Southern California, and my mother lived in Northern Oregon. One evening my father came to me waving a piece of paper in his hand; he indicated that the paper brought the news that "your mother died today." I got the impression that she died from the flu. My father turned away and left the room. I was left with my feelings.
>
> It was clear to me that my feelings were not to be talked about, so I left the house and spent an hour or so in an outbuilding with my dog, Captain Jiggs, crying and talking with him about how I felt. As nearly as I can remember, my father never mentioned my mother again. I didn't learn until I was seventeen that my mother had committed suicide, and this was learned from an aunt who, for some reason, was expressing her anger about my mother at the time. Once again, the information was just dumped, and there was no plan to talk with me about it. How did my mother die? Why did she die? What was the real truth? Why didn't anyone want to talk to me about it? My pain got buried under my confusion.

When we approach children openly and do our best to relate the experience of loss to something they already know about, or describe what is happening in language that matches their understanding, they will absorb the experience in the same way as any other new experience.

CONVERSATIONS WITH CHILDREN

A child's developmental level varies roughly with age. So does his/her interest and/or need to know more about a particular situation. Here's an example of some common conversations Peter has had with kids of different ages. Subject: his use of a wheelchair.

Two-year-old child: Points, looks at parent, and tries out words, "Da," "Look," "Bike," or something similar.

P: "Right, that's really good talking."

Three-year-old child: "What's that thing?" pointing at my chair, and looking to me for an answer.

P: "This is a chair I use to go places, kind of like a bike."

Child: "Oh." (Turns to parent.) "He has a bike; just like Billy?"

Four-year-old child: "Why do you have to use that chair?"

P: "Because I had a sickness that took my walking away."

Child: (Turns to parent) "Mom, he had a sickness that took his walking away. (Turns to me,) Didn'cha?"

P: "That's right."

Five to seven-year-old child: "Why do you have to use a wheelchair?"

P: "Because I had a sickness that took my walking away."

Child: "What kind of sickness?"

P: "A sickness called polio."

Child: "How'd ja get that?"

P: "Well, I just got sick one day, kind of felt like I had the 'flu'."

Child: "Could I get that?"

P: "No, I don't think so, because they've got a medicine now that you take to keep from getting this sickness; it's called the polio vaccine. I'll bet you've had that."

Younger kids may lose interest at this point. Older kids may follow that last conversation with other questions or remembrances of getting the vaccine, or they'll tell me of someone else they know who uses a wheelchair, or, often enough, they will add that a person they knew who used a wheelchair has died. I generally ask a child who has shared something like that how s/he felt about that happening, but whether or not I follow it out any further depends on the nature of my involvement. A lot of these conversations take place on the street or in a store where I don't know the child or parents, so I don't feel free to pursue the child's feelings.

Sometimes a child is referred to me because s/he is having trouble with or is disruptive in school. In that instance, I can follow up the clues a child offers about what might be going on underneath the behavior. For example:

> I was once asked to see a nine-year-old who had lost an eye. His mom said, "It's no problem; he never talks about it." At my suggestion that he "draw a picture of himself," he first drew a head-and-shoulders self-portrait. He drew this in full profile, with careful coloring and a good rendition of his hair style and a black eye-patch over the eye that he had lost. When I asked him to "tell me the story" of his drawing, he very quickly began to reveal the difficulty he was having with other kids who "made fun" of him because he had lost his eye. This opened the way for us to talk about all his feelings about the loss, which he did without reservation.

THREE-YEAR-OLD WITNESSES ACCIDENTAL DEATH

The following narrative is offered as an example of how to talk to a child who has witnessed a tragedy. It is offered here with the permission of Jennifer, Peter's daughter, and Annie Sparks, Sarah's mother, who, along with us, would like to support the full disclosure of events to children who may seem "too young" to know the facts. Due to the nature of this incident, you may be deeply affected. Your feelings are natural and expected. They are your feelings, present because you, too, have sustained some loss, and any deeply personal story can reawaken your sorrow.

The event happened in Berkeley, California, in 1973.

> "Sarah got hit by a truck," Jennifer says, her big eyes seeming to look to me for some way out of her pain and bewilderment. "I know," I say, holding her close to me and holding in as closely my own feelings of fear and sadness. "Can you tell me how that happened?"

So began the dialogue with my thirty-nine-month-old daughter, Jennifer, who just three hours earlier had seen her twenty-one-month-old friend, Sarah, hit, crushed, and thrown about by a large delivery truck making a U-turn in the intersection near our home. An hour earlier, I had tried to question Jennifer, but she had screamed, "Don't say it!" at me, retreating to her bed and sleep.

Now she was back and ready to talk to me.

J: Sarah and I were riding our bikes on the side-walk. . .

P: I see, and what else happened? (My heart was pounding, but I was determined to maintain a consistent, calm expression so that Jennifer could tell the whole story without distraction.)

J: Sarah and I were riding our bikes and we rode down to Mrs. D's house (the home of a friend who lived two houses down the street, on the corner).

P: OK, and what else?

J: Sarah and I were riding our bikes, and we rode down to Mrs. D's house, and we went around the corner . . . (a sob and an edge of fear in her voice now).

P: And what then?

J: Sarah and I rode down to Mrs. D's house, and we went around the corner, and we stopped at the "drive-way" (a boundary she had been taught to honor).

P: That was good, and what else?

J: Sarah and I went around the corner, and stopped at the driveway, and then we turned around to come back.

P: OK, and what else?

J: Sarah and I stopped at the driveway, and we turned around, and then we rode to the corner (her voice rising into a higher level of fear now).

P: All right. . .and what then?

J: Sarah and I turned around, and started riding, and Sarah was on this side of me" (indicating the street side).

P: I see, and what then?

J: Sarah and I were riding, and Sarah was on this side of me, and we got to the corner, and Sarah was too close to the street.

P: I see; so what happened?

J: Sarah and I. . . , we got to the corner, and Sarah was too close to the street, and Sarah's bike tipped off the curb.

P: Oh my; and what happened next?

J: And Sarah was too close to the street, and her bike fell off the curb, and Sarah fell down.

P: Yes, and what next?

J: And Sarah's bike tipped over, and Sarah fell down and I tried to reach her (gesturing to show her reaching for Sarah).

P: And then what?

J: And Sarah fell down, and I couldn't reach her, and the truck runned over her (very agitated now).

P: Oh, Jen. What else?

J: And the truck runned over her, and her mommy screamed, and I got scared.

P: Yes, it's very scary. . .and what happened then?

J: And her mommy screamed, and the truck didn't stop, and her mommy screamed, "Stop the truck! Stop the truck!" (Jennifer is screaming now.)

J:. . .and the truck didn't stop, and her mommy screamed more, "Stop the truck!" (Jennifer is screaming again.)

P: Yes, what happened next?

J: . . .and her mommy runned after the truck and banged on it, screaming, "Stop the truck!"

P: And what happened to Sarah?

J: Sarah went like this (started acting out flopping down on the floor and rolling over). And then she went like this (bouncing up again, flipping over, then falling down and then lying still).

P: What else do you remember?

J: And then the red snakes came.

P: Jen, where did the red snakes come from?

J: They comed out of Sarah's nose, and they went down into the street. (She said she was frightened of this.)

P: That must have been some of Sarah's blood coming out of her nose, and so she must have been hurt real bad like your thumb was hurt. Do you remember that?

J: Yes, and blood comed out of my thumb, too.

P: Yes, it was hurt real bad. Can you tell me anything more?

J: (Talks about the commotion and the police coming and her mom coming out and getting her.)

P: Is there anything more you want to tell me about it?

J: (Repeats the acting out of Sarah falling off the curb, and a truck hitting her, bouncing her, hitting her again, throwing her down again, and Sarah lying real still and the red snakes coming and says, "That must be Sarah's blood, huh.")

She then climbed into my lap where she cried for a while. I asked if there was anything more she wanted to tell me, and she shook her head "no." She was very tired then and ready to go to bed again.

I had had no time to cancel a group that was scheduled for that night, and toward the end of my time with Jennifer, people had begun to arrive (my office was behind my home).

I went out to the office and told the people in my group that I wanted their help this evening; I asked for time to share my feelings—feelings I had held back while Jennifer talked. They were very willing to give me the time. Everybody in the group knew Jennifer and Sarah. Everyone was deeply moved by the tragedy and supportive of my sharing of my feelings in the ways I had been asking them to do with the feelings they brought to group.

When I came back in the house from group, I learned that Sarah had died of her injuries. Given the description of her injuries, I had not expected her to survive, but this was the first official word of her death. We were all deeply saddened and outraged and convinced that we must encourage Jennifer to talk as much as she wanted to about her feelings.

Several days later, Jennifer and her mom came to me to talk about how angry Jennifer was that the doctors couldn't keep Sarah from dying. It was hard for her to know what "dying" really meant, and so I talked to her about it.

P: There are some things that doctors are able to fix

and some things that doctors aren't able to fix. Can you remember when your thumb was crunched in the car door when you were only two?

J: (Nodding her head, remembering, looking at her thumb.)

P: Remember that your mom took you to the hospital, and your doctor was able to fix your thumb so that it was able to work for you even though it still has some scars on it?

J: Yes, and the doctors made you better, too (referring to my use of a wheelchair), so why can't they make Sarah better?

P: But when I had the sickness that took my walking away, it was my arms and legs, not my head, that was hurt. The doctors were not able to fix my legs so they could work again, but they did fix me up so I could use a wheelchair, and I could still talk and go to work and be a daddy. Sarah's injuries were to her head, and the doctors couldn't fix that; Sarah wouldn't have been able to talk to you, or see you, or hear you, or play with you anymore. If it had only been her legs that they couldn't fix, she wouldn't have died, and she still would have been able to talk to you and play with you. But, with her head hurt the way it was, the doctors couldn't fix that. Her sickness was an injury that took away her talking, her hearing, her breathing, her smiling, her walking; it took away everything, and that's what dying is. (My tears begin to flow.) I feel very sad about this, and angry too, Jennifer, that Sarah has died.

J: (Crying and also making angry noises and gestures, as if not wanting to hear this.)

A month or so later, Jennifer and her mom had a brief interchange which illustrates the "magical thinking" basis for the guilt that sometimes arises around catastrophic loss. They were crossing a busy street on the way to the library. As they stopped for the traffic, Jen's mom stepped between Jennifer and the curb. Jennifer looked up and asked, "Why are you standing in front of me?"

"I just don't want you to be so close to the cars," replied her mom.

Jennifer thought for a moment and then asked, "If I had been in front of Sarah, Sarah wouldn't have gotten hit by the truck, would she?" Her mom acknowledged that that might be true, but didn't pursue the further implication that Jennifer may have been the one to be killed.

In the early period following Sarah's death, Jennifer continued to speak openly about her feelings and did not manifest any other difficulties associated with Sarah's death. She remained friends with Sarah's family, and even now, at age eighteen, she is still close to them.

When you talk with children about loss, it is important to enable them to relate the current loss to some other loss or change that they have experienced. This is always easier if it happens to be your child because you have an overview of all that your child has experienced, especially if your child is young. Everybody has lost something during his/her lifetime; even two- or three-year-old children can experience loss: a piece of clothing that was lost or worn-out; a toy that was lost or broken; a doll that was lost or broken beyond repair or just worn out; a family pet that they saw when injured or dead; some other animal they were familiar with that they have seen in death. Any of these may serve as an example for the child to understand the new experience of loss. If you don't know about the child's experience, you can ask the child: "Have you ever lost something you really cared about? Like a toy or a doll?"

An experience of the death of an animal is especially useful when a child must confront the death of someone s/he loves. A child can understand the profound change that is death when it is compared to a similar change in an animal that has died. A child can understand that a bird has certain characteristics: it flies, it sings or whistles, it perches in trees, it is bird. A child also can understand when seeing a dead bird that it has changed: it can't fly anymore; it can't sing anymore; it can't perch in trees anymore; it can't even move out of your hand; it isn't bird anymore; its body is dead. With this as basic information, the child can come to understand that his/her grandparent, brother, sister, mom, or dad has changed profoundly and can't be with him/her in the way s/he used to be. Understanding that such a loss has occurred will be the opening for the child's grief to begin to flow, and it will include the sadness, anger, and fears common to all grief. It will flow naturally if encouraged when it arises and if no explanations are used that the child just can't understand. You can deal with spirit in accordance with your own familial or religious beliefs. At the least, it consists of the collection of memories a small child has of the person s/he has lost. The workbook section will focus on preparing you to talk with your child, or other children, about loss.

THE WORKBOOK:
YOUR CHILDHOOD EXPERIENCES OF LOSS

UPDATING YOUR EXPERIENCES OF LOSS

In your journal, make a column headed "age" and fill in your ages from birth to the present time. Next to each age, list all the losses you can remember from birth to the present time. If you've been told of a significant loss which you don't remember, put it in with parentheses. Then, in the space that's left, make note of what feelings you had and what others' reactions were to the event or your feelings. This may fill several pages. Here's an example:

Age	Loss	Feelings
Birth	(Hard birth)	
1	(Parents separate.)	(I wouldn't eat, wanted daddy.)
2	(Go to live with dad; separate from sister.)	(Ate better; gained weight; missed sister.)
3		
4		
5		
6	Father remarries. I leave grandparents' home.	Sad, puzzled about new life.
7		
8	We fly to California; my dog dies en-route.	Sad, angry; I don't believe story of dog's death.
9		
10	Mother dies.	Father won't talk; I cry with my new dog; nobody talks to me about it; I feel alone and weird.

And so on. As feelings come up for you, continue to work through them as you did in the sections about sadness, anger, and fear.

YOUR CHILD'S EXPERIENCES OF LOSS:
(or a child you know well)
Make a similar page in your journal:

Age	Loss	Feelings
Birth	Labor stopped in hospital; doctor left; father left; nurses not believing mother; rushed delivery; strange doctor.	
1		
2	JFK assassinated.	Mother despondent for days, child confused, moody, sad.
3	Move to another city.	Child angry, defecating in pants frequently.
4	Pre-school.	Happy and productive away from home.
5	Kindergarten.	Happy.
6	In school all day; mother back in school (not so available).	Independent, moody.
7	Parents fighting.	Hiding, moody.
8	Good teacher; parents fighting.	Very happy at school.
9	4-H activities, friends, pets. Parents fighting.	Busy, happy with friends, moody.
10	Getting into trouble at school; mischievous. Mom is ally.	Feeling humiliated; gaining weight; close to mother.

11	Problem with teacher; changed class; kids gossiping.	Felt betrayed, humiliated; long talks with mother.
12	Began junior high. Parents leave country house and move into town; mother teaches junior high.	Nervous, excited; proud of mother, many friendships.
13	Parents divorce.	Angry, sad, fearful, relieved.
14	Become Dad's main helper.	Proud, resentful.
15	Came to live with Mom.	Fearful, happy, guilty.
16	Mom meets new partner.	Angry, resentful, curious.
17	Mom gets married.	Happy.
17	Comes to live with Mom, step dad.	Happy.
18	Goes to college.	Happy.

NOTES

CHAPTER NINE

The Death of Your Animal/Companion

As a final chapter to this book, we wanted to share our reflections on expressions of grief as they relate to the death of an animal that has been a part of your life. A friend who read the early manuscript expressed concern that the inclusion of grief about an animal might trivialize a profound loss such as the loss of a child.

As we talked about this, we realized that the larger danger is in trivializing grief no matter what it is about. In addition, we know that children benefit from having their grief about the loss of an animal fully and completely acknowledged. This is early training for acknowledging the grief they inevitably will encounter later in life.

It will come as no surprise that many people have as their primary companion an animal that provides affection and reason-for-being and asks little more than a square meal in return. For these people, the loss of a valued pet can be as profound as the loss of a mate.

Our journal notes illustrate the grieving process that followed the death of our two-year-old cat, Abe. It also represents the first time time that I, Zeva, experienced grieving with another person on a mutual, peer level. Peter and I supported each other's feelings; we were close without smothering each other.

Zeva's journal:
Last night, at 12:30 a.m., my son Daniel awakened us to

say that something terrible had happened. "Abe, or what is left of him, is in a box on the porch. I found him on the road; apparently someone was driving too close to the side of the road . . . right near our driveway."

The deep sleep state I was in wouldn't allow the truth to penetrate. Abe was the finest, fiercest cat, the most loyal and swift . . . he was so quick . . . No, not Abe. Abe was much too young; it wasn't time for him. He hadn't even come into his prime. Abe was a favorite among our clients . . . he would pick out the people who were the neediest . . . no matter where we were on the property . . . he would find a lizard and deposit it at our feet, a gesture that everyone always took to mean that they were noticed and loved. I remember when a bat flew into the stable-made-into-office; the women in my group were terrified. Abe, you came in and with one leap captured the bat in mid-air, taking it outside. I remembered the "Saturday-night mouse" you waited for; Jennifer loved your antics. When the mouse got away (you were such a ham that you often lost sight of him), you would sit for hours, looking so sad . . . No, it can't be you that is dead . . . .

Peter held me close through the night. Dreams of disbelief . . . it wasn't really Abe, but another cat that wasn't even hurt that badly. Relief . . . it was a nightmare! Shattered by the early morning awakening that brought the realization, the awareness, that it was Abe, I found myself writing furiously. Anger . . . rage . . . at the careless driver, at the road itself that deceived us by saying "Not a Through Street" and then turned out to be a monstrous speedway at times. Sadness and an incredible outpouring of tears. Peter was silent. I felt a tug at the comforter . . . just like the feeling of Abe on our bed. Relief again . . . Abe was back. I slowly allowed my hand to travel to the place I felt the tug. It was Peter's hand, wrapped around his head. He was startled . . . feeling my hand but thinking that it, too, was Abe. We shared our reactions and found that we both were in the same place with our grief. We got up and went outside together and confirmed that it was, indeed, our Abe, and he was dead.

We mutely fixed and ate breakfast, not really knowing what we were eating. I sat down with my journal and every book in the house on loss, death, dying, poetry, animals.

Someone might say something that applied to Abe, and I wanted to collect all relevant thoughts. I wrote what seemed appropriate. . . .

> "I leave no trace of wings in the air,
> But I'm glad I had my flight."

I wrote letters to all the people we knew who loved Abe, including the above quotation. I needed everyone to know how much I was grieving.

Peter joined me. He had his journal as well, and we wrote independently. Sometimes I looked at him as the tears streamed down his face, and I wondered what he was thinking. Sometimes I asked, and I shared my thoughts. We were separate in our writing, but together in our grief: the loss was mutual; we knew how much we cared, and we knew our pain and sadness were in direct relationship to how much we cared for Abe.

We did not call Jennifer immediately. We knew that she would be home alone, and we wanted to wait until her mother was there so she could comfort Jen directly. We arranged to pick her up from school in Berkeley at noon on Friday instead of having her take the bus as planned on Saturday. We wanted her with us when we buried Abe. We didn't want him to simply disappear out of her life; she needed to see that Abe was dead, and she was the one to choose a burial place for him.

Peter read his journal notes at the funeral:
Abe (April 1979 to April 1981)
You found us in a campground, you and your brother, and when we let you know we wanted you to come live with us, you and "Obie" ran off into the woods. . .as if to check out our sincerity. The person we had visited in the campground convinced you to stick around the next day until Zeva could get out there to pick you both up, and you came to live at Wintercreek on July 28, 1979. You were about three months old then.

You were more independent than Obie, less likely to approach strangers and make overtures for affection, which might be why Obie disappeared when you were about six months old. We could find no trace of him, nor could you point out anything, even though we coaxed and followed you. You and he had been so close, so caring for each other, that we were certain that if he'd been injured and was around, you'd lead us to him. . . but nothing.

Your grief, disorientation, and aimlessness in the days that followed were obvious, and you allowed us to be closer to you than before, and gradually you transferred your trust, caring, loyalty, and affection to us and Wintercreek.

You came running to meet us when we returned after being away, began to bring us the prizes from your hunting, and were always ready for some holding and loving; and you returned that with unswerving affection.

You were delighted when Jennifer and I made your cat-door in the barn so that you could go in and out independently. No, you never gave up your independence. You simply expanded your world to include us. When we moved to the house in April, 1980, it was not new for you, but we were very slow to build you an entrance you could use independently, and so our relationship was different. You tolerated having to ring the bells to come in, or talk to us about getting out, but you remained affectionate and loyal and patient.

You began to involve yourself in our work with people in your own way: gently, in an unassuming way, sharing your warmth or affection with people who, at that point in their lives, were believing themselves unworthy of giving or receiving any warmth or affection and unable to allow us to reach out to them. You could find us anywhere, and would climb into the lap of the person we were working with, settle in, and begin your deep rumbling purr, and they would begin to respond to you and to their own need to be close.

After we finished your cat-door and cat-walk into the house, you quickly returned to your way of coming and going independently, and your pleasure was unmistakable. After a night of hunting, you would come in and sleep quietly at the edge of our bed, very careful not to disturb us. Sometimes as we would awaken to watch the sunrise brush the trees with gold, you, too, would awaken and watch out the window. We wondered what you were thinking. As often as not, as we'd begin to stir, you'd climb onto our chests, give us a kiss, and begin to purr strongly. . .just being close. Then, as we'd begin to get up, you'd talk to us about getting you some food, or wanting some loving, or ask, "Who is this new person staying here?"

I cherished your way of including others in your world. I admired and envied your ability to go gracefully and without fear into the woods. I admired your strength and ability as a hunter. Even though it saddened me when you would bring a squirrel into the kitchen, I was touched by your sharing and knew that if we were hungrier, you'd have given us your catch without a quarrel. I admire and envy your way of being in the world, and I hope that I can achieve a way that is similar in nature.

Last night you were struck down in the road by a two-legged person whose way is not gentle. Daniel found you and brought you home in a box. I've touched your body and know you are dead, but still feel your strength. I am deeply hurt by your wounds and your death. I want you back, alive and strong. I know you have ceased to exist in that way. I want your spirit to remain among us always. I pray I am worthy of that.

Soon we will give your body back to the earth. You will always be the fine, fierce cat I love dearly. Go well, good friend.

THE WORKBOOK:
JOURNAL WRITING ABOUT GRIEF

Whatever loss you are writing about, you may want to write more about your feelings in journals or letters, using prose or poetry. Begin your work by using the same techniques of relaxation and conscious breathing; take the time and space to create the atmosphere for your work. We suggest that you write freely and often and share your writing with others. Any unexpressed feeling will flow into your writing. The more you write, the more there will be a sense of completion.

Avoid questions such as "Why did this happen?" "Will I ever feel better?" State your feelings and thoughts. "I'm angry this happened." "I want to get through this loss and feel better about myself." Be as specific as possible.

NOTES

Epilogue

We've written this book at a compelling time: Vietnam Vets are coming out of hiding; AIDS is upon us—all of us; slaughter on the highways continues to take lives, and we are no healthier or better able to deal with loss than we were in 1976 when the paper "Emotional Responses to Loss in the Newly Disabled Adult" was presented.

No matter how well prepared you are for the death of someone you care about, the death, when it occurs, still will bring a measure of grief with it. Even in the situation of severe chronic debilitating illness, such as Alzheimer's disease and AIDS, where there might be an element of relief that the dying person is finally released from the discomfort, pain, and confusion of the long illness, you can expect grief to follow, as well as a certain amount of guilt as the backlash to any relief.

We who work with grief must be prepared to have our own sense of loss re-stimulated by the work of others. We don't believe that it is possible to be truly objective in doing this work with grief. We are dealing here with a subjective experience, one so fraught with feeling that we must be moved by it. We must be prepared for this by being as up-to-date as possible with our own grief work, being prepared to do more of our own work if we begin to become immersed in the grief of others. Be aware, however, that there are "pockets of grief" that can exist, unknown to you, for years. If you are in a situation of frequently "being there" for others, you will, most certainly, have to put your feelings away for a while, and these feelings go into the "pockets," waiting for the opportunity to be experienced. In the writing of this book, the stored grief came up in waves; some of it was predictable, such as the feelings that are in response to Sarah's death. We probably always will have deep sorrow when we think of that experience. You may experience a "pocket of grief" with just the idea that some parents take time to talk with a child about loss. If your parents never knew how to do that, and did not take the time to find out how to respond, you may find yourself experiencing grief about that. One of the examples referred to here was about Jennifer's having badly injured her thumb when she was two. We were looking for an example of a "wound," and Peter dictated the history of that incident. By the time he was half-way into the story, deep sobs filled his chest. For fifteen years, that pocket of grief stayed buried. That's what happens when you put your own feelings aside (which we encourage you to do when responding to children) and don't experience the grief soon after the event.

Our lives are so busy that most of us don't take the time at the end of the day to do an "inventory" of the day's events, seeing if there is some feeling left over from the day we need to acknowledge. We would be healthier, more centered, and better able to assist others if we did put this kind of acknowledgment high on our priority list. Forms of meditation, journal writing, talking/sharing at the dinner table, letting the feelings come up to be acknowledged—any or all of these activities are mandatory in the lives of helping professionals and lay people.

It is probably clear by now that we don't support the myth about being "objective" in the face of tragedy. Do your own work; be clear and up-to-date about your own losses. If feelings come up in the time you take with another person, acknowledge them, and they will subside for the moment. They won't stop you from listening to your (friend) (client) (patient) (child) (partner) (parent) (sibling). Remember to breathe to reduce your own stress response, and later make time to write in your journal. Share your feelings with someone who will support your grief. We guarantee that you will have the energy and spirit to continue working with others.

Suggested Reading

Cohen, Marion Deutsche. *An Ambitious Sort of Grief*. Texas: Ide House, Inc., 1983. A helpful book for bereaved parents, especially for those who lose a child at birth or shortly thereafter. Simply written.

Davies, Phyllis. *Grief: Climb Toward Understanding*. New Jersey: Lyle Stuart Inc., 1988. The author, using writing as a tool for healing her grief, has compiled her own poetry in response to her teen-aged son's death. In addition, she offers a "check-list" with the difficult but necessary steps to take following a death.

Isle, Sherokee. *Empty Arms*. Minnesota: self-published, 1982. A guide to help parents cope with miscarriage, stillbirth, and neonatal loss. Very warm and simply written.

Kubler-Ross, Elizabeth, M.D. *On Death and Dying*. New York: Macmillan Publishing Company, 1970. The pioneering book on this difficult subject.

_____ *On Children and Death*. New York: Macmillan Publishing Company, 1983. An inspirational book that aids families of dying children. Warm and simple language.

Levine, Stephen. *Who Dies?* New York: Anchor Press/Doubleday, 1982. An investigation of conscious living and conscious dying. Addresses many aspects of the dying process with insight and compassion.

_____ *Healing Into Life and Death*. New York: Anchor Press/Doubleday, 1987. Offers original techniques for working with pain and grief. Healing meditations.

Miller, Alice. *Drama of the Gifted Child*. New York: Basic Books, 1981. Every sentence in this slim text contains a powerful message. Don't let the analytical terms discourage you. Dr. Miller clearly states that the dysfunctional patterns of the family of origin can be broken through a constructive grieving process.

_____ *For Your Own Good: Hidden Cruelty in Child-Rearing and the Roots of Violence*. Canada: McGraw-Hill/Ryerson Limited, 1983. Dr. Miller takes on the challenge of the roots of violence and the devastating effect on children.

_____ *Thou Shalt Not Be Aware: Society's Betrayal of the Child*. New York: Meridian, 1986. Dr. Miller relies on her first two books to support the theory she puts forth in this book. She offers an understanding in confronting and treating the devastation of child abuse. A must for therapists from dysfunctional families.

_____ *Pictures of a Childhood*. Canada: Collins Publishers, 1986. The fourth in a series of books that address hostility and abuse toward children. This book, the most personal of the four, is a collection of paintings done by the author. There is very little theory, but the connection between the traumas of childhood and creative expression is made.

Palmer, Laura. *Shrapnel in the Heart*. New York: Random House, Inc., 1987. A collection of heartrending letters-to-the-dead left at the Vietnam Veterans Memorial in Washington, D.C., and compassionate interviews with some of the families/friends who left them.

Pelletier, Kenneth. Mind as Healer, Mind as Slayer. New York: Dell Publishing Co., Inc., 1977. A classic study of the relationship of mind to body, and stress to physical illness.

_____ *Holistic Medicine*. New York: Delacorte Press/Seymour Lawrence, 1979. A synthesis of the author's ideas into a plan for achieving optimum health through the utilization of stress-control techniques, nutrition practices and exercise.

Pearce, Joseph Chilton. *Magical Child*. New York: Bantam Books, Inc., 1980. A sensitive and refreshing new look at early childhood development and the unlimited potential of every child's intellect.

_____ *Magical Child Matures*. New York: Bantam Books, Inc., 1986. An extension of the author's ideas to encompass the effect of adolescent development on adult life.

Rossi, Ernest. *The Psychobiology of Mind-Body Healing*. New York: W. W. Norton & Company, Inc., 1986. A scholarly text that helps explain how stress can contribute to debilitating illness. New approaches to mind/body healing are introduced.

Endnotes

1. Leech, Peter. *The Emotional Responses to Loss in the Newly Disabled Adult.* Berkeley, California: The Wright Institute, 1976.

2. Fankhauser, Jerry, M.S.W. "The Whirlpool Experience". *From a Chicken to an Eagle (What Happens When You Change).* Houston, Texas.

3. References in Chapter Two regarding children following models were taken from a lecture given by Joseph Chilton Pearce. Sonoma State University, Rohnert Park, California: March, 1985.

Letters

In the first printing of our book, we asked for responses and suggestions from our readers. We decided to share some of those responses in this second printing of *ACKNOWLEDGMENT: Opening to the Grief of Unacceptable Loss*.

"I have just finished *ACKNOWLEDGMENT*. It is an amazingly powerful book and good reading as well. Upon completion of your book, my stomach tightened, my throat lumped, and tears welled over various primary losses and my inability to deal with them. My immediate reaction, of course, was to subdue these feelings because I didn't want to deal with them at the moment. (A more accurate assessment is that is how I was taught to deal with my emotional expression.) I think, with the help of your book, I can acquire my feelings and start expressing emotions, thereby dealing with the losses in my life rather than leaving them covered by the bandages that hide the wounds. I am feeling better just knowing that I want to do something about it. Thanks for the enlightenment from *ACKNOWLEDGMENT*."
Keith Pomeroy, Chico State University, Chico, California

"My client had been to see me several times and told me she had been fired from her job but placed no special emphasis on that information. She talked of several problems but seemed to go nowhere, nor did I! There was no pressing immediate problem, only a malaise, a dissatisfaction, a sense of "lostness." (As I reviewed) your book, I began to see how her loss might be a serious problem for her. When I acknowledged to her how deep her loss must have been to her, a floodgate opened. Her first response was relief. . . She did all the exercises, and when she acknowledged the companion losses that went with the job loss, she began to find a measure of relief and belief that she could go back to living a 'real life.'

I learned from this book and became a more sensitive listener, and my client has something tangible and constructive to help her work through her unacceptable loss. Thank you for writing this book; it has helped me as a therapist, and it has liberated my client."

Sincerely, Beth Smyth, Marriage/Family Therapist

As a former coordinator of Compassionate Friends of Ukiah and Willits, California, I am recommending this dynamic, highly innovative approach to a very painful subject. I think it will be helpful for anyone who has lost a child. Fifteen years down the road, I am still discovering things that I need to deal with regarding my son's death. Peter and Zeva's approach has helped me a great deal.

Sincerely, Bernie Crews

STUDENT COMMENTS:
"This book helped me to thoroughly grieve my loss. I have come away feeling empowered and released from my pain."

Margaret O'Neill

"*ACKNOWLEDGMENT* helped me take the necessary time to realize my losses and to grieve and grow in new and different ways. It is an extraordinary book."

Debbie Shuster

"As I found my pain, I uncovered my joy as well. *ACKNOWLEDGMENT* not only opened up a part of my life, (but also) the feelings that my five-year-old feels and can now more easily share with me."

Veronica Fisher

"The importance of the book to me was the statement that there were losses that were unacceptable. This 'permission granted' gave me the freedom to put an amount of closure on my unacceptable loss. (This) was very helpful.

Bonnie Ruther

"It enriches my (limited) knowledge about losses. I thought I was handling my losses well until I read. . .*ACKNOWLEDGMENT*. . .been keeping it all to myself thinking I was so different and weird."

Angelina Baustista

"This book is truly excellent. It helped me. . .get in touch with myself and (helped) me. . .understand my feelings. Thanks for a wonderful book."

Joycelyn Y. Teague

"In the book *ACKNOWLEDGMENT*, I especially appreciated the focus on 'Childhood Experience of Loss.' I'm a clearer, more complete person as a result! I (also) enjoyed the 'Focusing on Fear' section. I was able to put my fears in the proper perspective and work on them."

(unsigned)

"*ACKNOWLEDGMENT* gives us the important information that many losses are unacceptable. The sanest approach to loss is sometimes, 'No, this is not acceptable.' I will not forget; (I will) get on with my life; I care, and I will grieve."

Dana VanderHorst

"Knowing that my losses are outrageous and unacceptable, because someone else smarter than I thinks so, too, was a great relief. (It) freed me to feel and let me open to my grief and, at least a little, to others. I gained comfort from knowing it is okay to be afraid."

(unsigned)

"I found in this book part of my life that I knew but was witholding in my mind. After the workbook assignments, I find myself greatly relieved. I, too, cried at some of the remembrances. Thank you for helping."

Charles W. Webster

FROM THE AUTHORS:
We are interested in the various ways this book is used. One therapist said she cut the book into chapters, giving her client one chapter a week. The exercises were done faithfully, and the client's depression lifted by the time she finished the book.

Taken chapter by chapter, the book offers a completely self-contained guide for groups as well as individuals. It is perfectly suited for group discussion and homework assignments.

Instructors have found it helpful as a companion text in classes that deal with the subject of loss, human emotions, and relationship transitions.

Due to the simple language and practical application of the theory, this book has been found to be age-appropriate for young people as well as for adults.

The next book in the *ACKNOWLEDGMENT* series will address specific issues of loss in depth, especially secondary loss. *Opening to the Grief* will remain the basic text and workbook.

Please continue to send suggestions and comments to:

Leech/Singer Associates
Box 885
Laytonville, California 95454
707/984-8224

WORKSHOPS, TRAININGS IN
THE *ACKNOWLEDGMENT APPROACH*
ARE AVAILABLE

To Order More Copies

If your local bookstore does not yet carry *ACKNOWLEDG-MENT*, you may avoid delay by ordering directly from Wintercreek Publications. Use the enclosed order form. Your bookstore may call us for the name of our distributor.

Gift books will be accompanied by a gift card at no extra charge. Remember to include any message you wish to have sent along with your name on the bottom of the order form.

ORDERING INFORMATION: All titles should be ordered through Wintercreek Publications.

INDIVIDUALS: Please include payment with your orders, adding postage and handling charges of $1.50 for the first book and 75¢ for each additional book, plus applicable sales tax.

TRADE RETAIL: Please call for information — 707/984-8224

ORDER FORM: All orders are payable in US currency only.
Foreign payment must be International Money Order.

Send to: **Wintercreek Publications, P.O. Box 1166, Laytonville, CA 95454**

	Price	Quan.	Amount
Name	@$9.95		
Address	California sales tax 6%		
City	postage & handling		
State ZIP	**enclose payment**		$

Send Brochure ☐   Gift Book ☐

To: _____
Name

_____
Address

_____
City

_____
State   ZIP

Gift Card Signed: _____

To Order More Copies

If your local bookstore does not yet carry *ACKNOWLEDG-MENT,* you may avoid delay by ordering directly from Winter-creek Publications. Use the enclosed order form. Your bookstore may call us for the name of our distributor.

Gift books will be accompanied by a gift card at no extra charge. Remember to include any message you wish to have sent along with your name on the bottom of the order form.

ORDERING INFORMATION: All titles should be ordered through Wintercreek Publications.

INDIVIDUALS: Please include payment with your orders, adding postage and handling charges of $1.50 for the first book and 75¢ for each additional book, plus applicable sales tax.

TRADE RETAIL: Please call for information—707/984-8224

ORDER FORM: All orders are payable in US currency only. Foreign payment must be International Money Order.

Send to: **Wintercreek Publications, P.O. Box 1166, Laytonville, CA 95454**

	Price	Quan.	Amount
Name	@$9.95		
Address	California sales tax 6%		
City	postage & handling		
State ZIP	**enclose payment**		$

Send Brochure ☐   Gift Book ☐

To: _____
    Name

_____
Address

_____
City

_____
State   ZIP

Gift Card Signed: _____